THE ILLUSION OF WAGE AND PRICE CONTROL

THE ILLUSION OF WAGE AND PRICE CONTROL

Essays on Inflation, its Causes and its Cures

Contributors include
DAVID LAIDLER, MICHAEL PARKIN, JACKSON GRAYSON;
MICHAEL WALKER (Editor)

THE FRASER INSTITUTE
1976

Canadian Cataloguing in Publication Data
Main entry under title:
The Illusion of wage and price control
  Includes bibliographical references.
  ISBN 0-88975-001-7 pa.
  ISBN 0-88975-005-X pa.

  1. Wage-price policy—Addresses, essays,
lectures. 2. Price regulation—Addresses, essays,
lectures. 3. Inflation (Finance)—Addresses,
essays, lectures. I. Walker, Michael, 1945-
II. Laidler, David E. W., 1938-   III. Parkin,
Michael, 1939-   IV. Grayson, Charles Jackson,
1923-
HC79.W24I45   332.4'1   C76-016012-0

First published 1976 by the Fraser Institute.
ISBN 0-88975-001-7 (Paperbound Edition)
ISBN 0-88975-005-X (Pocketbook Edition)
COPYRIGHT CANADA, ALL RIGHTS RESERVED.
Manuscripts processed and set by K. Hay at the Fraser Institute.
Printed in Canada.

Contents

PART II — HAVE CONTROLS EVER WORKED?

THE HISTORICAL RECORD: A SURVEY OF WAGE AND PRICE CONTROLS OVER FIFTY CENTURIES

Robert L. Schuettinger

THE POST-WAR RECORD:
WAGE AND PRICE CONTROLS:
THE LESSONS FROM BRITAIN

Michael Parkin

THE POST-WAR RECORD:
THE U.S. ECONOMIC STABILIZATION
PROGRAM OF 1971-1974

Michael R. Darby

THE POST-WAR RECORD:
A VIEW FROM THE OUTSIDE
OF THE INSIDE
OF UPSIDE DOWN

Jackson Grayson

PART III — WHAT IS THE SOLUTION?
AN ALTERNATIVE TO WAGE AND PRICE CONTROLS

David Laidler

PART IV — INFLATION DIALOGUE
SOME QUESTIONS AND ANSWERS ABOUT INFLATION

Michael Walker

Preface

The purpose of this Institute publication is to present a series of essays on inflation, wage and price controls and the cure for inflation. Contributors to this volume were invited during September and October 1975 to write papers drawing on their detailed research into these matters. Each of the authors brings to this volume a special expertise in the area upon which he has written. Jack Carr of the University of Toronto, who has written the first essay, was invited to write about the causes of inflation, the role that prices play in the economic life of the country and the effect that controls have on both inflation and upon the functioning of Canada's market economy. Professor Carr brings to the volume a wide-ranging experience in research in this area including extensive research into the causes of inflation that he did for the 'old' Prices and Incomes Commission.

Talking about something is no substitute for doing it and in his essay Professor Jackson Grayson, who was the price controller in Phase Two of President Nixon's price control programme, provides a first hand account of what it was like to control wages and prices. In some sense, Grayson's essay is the most important one in the book because it lays bare the human side of the economic controls that he attempted to administer.

Wage and price controls appear to be one of mankind's oldest responses to inflation. In a review of the historical record, Robert Schuettinger finds that controls are literally as old as civilization itself.† Not surprisingly, controls in Canada and the U.S. came early in the history of both these countries. What is surprising is the early date at which some observers realized what the true cause of inflation is.

---

†We are indebted to the Heritage Foundation for permission to reprint substantial portions of their Policy Study Number 2, *A Brief Survey of Price and Wage Controls From 2800 B.C. to A.D. 1952*, Robert L. Schuettinger, Washington, D.C., 1974.

Wage and price controls as a modern peace time policy were first extensively adopted in the United Kingdom. The first in-depth attempt to analyze wage and price controls as applied in the United Kingdom was done in 1970 by Professor Michael Parkin, together with Professor Richard Lipsey. Professor Parkin was asked to provide for this volume an opinion as to whether or not wage and price controls have worked in the United Kingdom. The set of economic circumstances arising in Canada are often referred to as the 'British disease'. The current wage and price control programme is very similar to programmes that have been tried in the United Kingdom and, in fact, bears the same name as the current wage and price control programme in the United Kingdom, *Attack on Inflation*; it is therefore particularly appropriate that Professor Parkin provide an analysis of the effect that these programmes have had in the United Kingdom.

Like Professor Parkin, Professor Michael Darby, from the University of California in Los Angeles, is a pioneer in analyzing the impact of wage and price controls in his country. Professor Darby kindly consented to provide for this volume a summary, a synthesis and an extension of his recent research into the effects of the wage and price control programme in the United States.

The most difficult task in this volume, that of providing an alternative to wage and price controls as a solution to the inflation problem, fell to Professor David Laidler of the University of Western Ontario. Professor Laidler is a widely respected academician, has taught at many universities in the United Kingdom and the United States and is an expert in monetary economics.

The last essay in the book is a summary in dialogue form of the principal points covered in the book. It uses the conclusions of the analysis contained in the studies to construct answers to some of the basic questions that people have about inflation and controls.

AN ANTI-INFLATION PROGRAMME

The studies in this volume provide all of the principles and most of the raw material from which to fashion an anti-inflation programme. The remainder of this preface is devoted to the development of a concrete anti-inflation alternative that draws on the contributions of the distinguished authors.

The money supply rule

In his study in this volume, Professor David Laidler develops the case for a money supply rule — why and how it will produce price stability. The purpose of this section is to provide a concrete proposal for action to implement Professor Laidler's suggestion.

Although the Bank of Canada is responsible for the day-to-day management of the money supply, the Bank of Canada Act (Section 14) very clearly specifies that the Minister of Finance is ultimately responsible for the activities of the Bank of Canada.† Accordingly, it is the Minister of Finance who is responsible for the rate at which the money supply grows.

As it is currently written, the Bank of Canada Act makes provision for a directive 'in specific terms' to be sent from the Minister of Finance to the Governor of the Bank of Canada only in the event that there is a difference of opinion about the conduct of monetary policy between the Minister and the Governor. Accordingly, although there are occasional public statements by the Governor of the Bank about the general course of monetary policy, there is seldom an explicit statement of the precise agreement between the Minister and the Governor about targets that the Bank is trying to achieve.

---

†Section 14(2) of the Bank of Canada Act states:

"If, notwithstanding the consultations provided for in subsection (1), there should emerge a difference of opinion between the Minister and the Bank concerning the monetary policy to be followed, the Minister may, after consultation with the Governor and with the approval of the Governor in Council (Ed.—the Cabinet), give to the Governor a written directive concerning monetary policy, in specific terms and applicable for a specified period, and the Bank shall comply with such directive."

In a recent speech,† the Governor of the Bank of Canada went farther than he has ever gone in detailing what he thought the Bank's target ought to be:

> "If the ultimate goal — the restoration of a completely stable price level, that is, a zero rate of inflation — is to be achieved, this will eventually require the maintenance of an average rate of growth of the money supply no higher than the long term average rate of growth of the production of goods and services in Canada — that is, a rate of about 5 per cent a year."

Having made this statement, which is entirely in agreement with Professor Laidler's, the Governor went on to subject it to a variety of qualifications. He also pointed out that it was difficult for central banks, like the Bank of Canada, to commit themselves to very specific targets. The reason he gave for this was that:

> "There are questions in our minds about how far we can properly rely on any one indicator to get a good reading of the thrust of our policy actions. Until we have had more experience with the problems encountered in trying to adhere to particular monetary growth targets, we will feel bound to regard such targets as tentative and subject to revision in light of developments that may not have been anticipated."

In other words, although the Bank of Canada judges that it ought to be keeping the rate of money creation at or near 5 per cent per annum, it does not have great confidence in that judgement. This uncertainty is reflected in the actual rates of growth of the money supply which have, on average, over the last five years been nearly three times higher than the target.

The objectives of the Bank of Canada, as set down in the preamble to the Bank of Canada Act, are vague and this lack of precision is reflected in the policy stance of the Bank. We could all feel more comfortable about the state of affairs

---

†Reported in the Bank of Canada Review, December 1975.

if the actual behaviour of the money supply and hence, monetary policy, were constantly being judged against a specific target. In more human terms, since the 'job description' of the Bank of Canada laid down in the Bank of Canada Act is as vague as, "to promote the economic and financial welfare of the Dominion", then how are we to know whether and to what extent it is doing the job properly? As long as the 'money supply rule' is rejected, neither we nor the Minister of Finance have a reasonable guide by which to measure the performance of monetary policy.

Accordingly, because it seems to be the only reasonable long term anti-inflation policy and because it makes a positive and precise assignment of responsibility for monetary policy, we suggest that the Department of Finance adopt the monetary rule suggested by Professor Laidler. We suggest that the move to the rule be made gradually and suggest the following interim targets for the total privately-held money supply:

1. For the year ending December 1976, growth at 11 per cent or a target not greater than $73,560 million.

2. For the year ending December 1977, growth at 8.5 per cent or a target not greater than $79,812 million.

3. For the year ending December 1978, growth at 7.5 per cent or a target not greater than $85,599 million.

4. For the year ending December 1979, growth at 6.0 per cent or a target not greater than $90,734 million.

In terms of implementation, we suggest the following:

1. That the Bank of Canada Act, Section 14(1), be amended as follows: Section 14(1) The Minister and the Governor shall consult regularly on monetary policy and on its *success in achieving a rate of monetary growth roughly equal to the long-term average rate*

of growth of the production of goods and services in Canada. As a result of these consultations, there shall be a public statement, at least once every quarter, as to the overall objectives of monetary policy for the three month and twelve month period following. This public statement shall be in the form of a target growth rate for the total deposits of those institutions covered by the provisions of the Bank Act and total currency held by the general public and shall be published in the Canada Gazette.

2. That to further the objective of control, the provisions of the Bank Act pertaining to the holding of cash reserves be extended to cover all institutions offering deposits subject to cheque and who, directly or indirectly, participate in the clearing system.

A programme to curtail government spending

If there is a case to be made for wage and price controls, it is that they have an effect on people's expectations. They are supposed to make people feel that the inflation rate will be lower in the future and encourage them to plan accordingly. The reason that controls are supposed to have that effect is that people are supposed to believe that controls will stop inflation. It follows from this that the key element in the success of wage and price controls is the extent to which people believe that the programme will be a success. In turn, a key aspect of general belief is obvious general support for the controls programme.

The latter precondition for success seems already to have been lost in the current anti-inflation campaign. Organized labour has vehemently opposed the controls from the start and although business has shown a willingness to 'live with' controls, the endorsement could hardly be described as enthusiastic. In short, the general attitude is to regard controls as an evil. The fact that maybe even as many as half the people also regard them as necessary and effective probably is not, in the face of the basic cynicism, enough to ensure that the programme will affect people's expectations.

Since the objective of a 'high profile' economic policy, like wage and price controls, is to affect people's attitudes, it seems clear that it would be wise to select a course of action for which there would be general support. Wage and price controls attempt to rally people around an attack on 'greed' — an attack that inevitably flounders in the infighting between unions, government and business.

It is our suggestion that the rallying point be an attack on the excessive growth in government expenditure — an attack that business, labour and the tax-paying public should be able to support. The main purpose of this section is to develop a clear-cut guideline that can serve as the focal point in an attack on government spending.

The target

In his address to the nation on October 13, 1975, the Prime Minister stated that it would not be possible to reduce government spending to the point where it was 'absolutely frozen':

> "Indeed it must increase if we are to continue to provide essential services, such as cushioning Canadians against part of the increase in the cost of imported oil, protecting the aged and others living on fixed incomes against some of the effects of inflation, and continuing to provide assistance to those who are unemployed."

Some four months later (February 19, 1976), the Federal government made available spending estimates that would involve an increase of about 18 per cent in its spending over the first fiscal year of the anti-inflation programme. In our estimation, this demonstrates a lack of sincerity on the part of the Federal government and reveals an inability on the part of the Treasury Board to control the spending of government departments. In a recent publication, the C.D. Howe Institute remarked that the reason for this apparent lack of discipline in government spending was that there did "not appear to be an incentive system that would encourage either the departmental officials or the Cabinet to be deeply concerned about the cost of a programme."† In other words,

---

†Judith Maxwell, *Policy Review and Outlook, 1975*, C.D. Howe Research Institute, 1975, p. 46.

government managers don't have a profit and loss statement to tell them when to expand and when to contract their programmes. It is not surprising, then, that vague promises by the Prime Minister to do something about government expenditure produce an increase of 18 per cent during the first year of the programme.

The immediate solution to this problem of uncontrollable spending is for governments at all levels to commit themselves to a strict expenditure guideline. The guideline should be made public and there should be frequent public reports on the degree of success in adhering to it. The following is the Fraser Institute's proposal along these lines:

1. The objective should be to freeze the number of cents out of each dollar that governments at all levels spend.

2. Therefore, the ultimate target for government spending ought to be about seven per cent growth per year. (5 per cent capacity real growth plus 2 per cent growth in prices. This target has already been adopted for defence spending.)

3. The immediate goal ought to be to reduce government spending by half the amount necessary to achieve the target. (In fiscal year 1976-1977, government expenditure ought to grow by no more than 11.5 per cent as opposed to the minimum current estimate of 16 per cent; in 1977-1978 the target should be 9.25 per cent growth; in 1978-1979 the target should be 7.75 per cent and in 1979-1980 the target should be 7 per cent.)

4. To implement this programme, the Federal and Provincial governments should set a guideline for each department and instruct each department to publish a quarterly statement of its expenditures. In that report, the department should demonstrate what is being done to ensure that the department is meeting the commitment to the guideline. Overshooting the

guideline should be regarded as a 'loss' and detailed documentation of the reasons for the loss should be provided. In other words, every government department should be subjected to the financial discipline of quarterly public reporting.

5. In conjunction with the establishment of the guideline, there should be established a Government Expenditures Review Board. This Board, appointed by the Governor in Council, should have terms of reference similar to the current Anti-Inflation Board, namely:

● monitoring movements in departmental spending in relation to the guidelines

● "identifying actual or proposed movements that would contravene the guideline in fact or in spirit"

● "endeavouring through consultations and negotiations with the parties involved to modify actual or proposed increases to bring them within the limits and spirit of the guideline..."

● "referring to an official with the authority of enforcement ... the actual or proposed movement ... if the consultations and negotiations do not lead to their modification; and"

● "promoting greater public understanding of the inflationary process by publishing reports, arranging public hearings and meetings, and by other means."†

In those cases where the guidelines will be or have been contravened, the Board should be empowered to order that:

● the department be enjoined from contravening or continuing to contravene the guidelines.

---

†*Attack on Inflation*, Policy statement tabled in the House of Commons by the Honourable Donald S. Macdonald, Minister of Finance, October 14, 1975.

6. In adjusting to the guideline, expenditure cuts should be made, to the extent possible, on goods and services items and not on payroll except where attrition warrants. In this way, the unemployment effects of government sector contraction would, to the extent that they occur, be more evenly distributed throughout the economy.

What about controls?

The conclusion of the studies in this volume is that controls are unlikely to work. In other countries, price freezes with wide-spread support (the U.S.) or voluntary restraint with rationing (the U.K.) have had a modest 'shock' effect, but no lasting effect on inflation. Since controls can have very substantial adverse side effects, the view of the authors is that wage and price controls should be dropped.

The view of the Fraser Institute is also that controls be dropped — however, to avoid the effects that sudden termination might have on people's expectations about inflation, it is proposed that the controls be dropped gradually and not until the public review of government expenditures has begun. Once the 'attack' on government expenditure has begun, the illusion that 'the government is doing something' — temporarily lost by the abandonment of controls — would be recreated. The advantage of using government expenditure as the "prop" in such an illusion is that the Federal Government's cash requirement would thereby be reduced. This fact would make the Bank of Canada's task of following the money supply guideline much easier than it would otherwise be.

PART I

setting the scene

Wage and Price Controls Panacea for Inflation or Prescription for Disaster?

JACK CARR

Associate Professor of Economics
University of Toronto
Visiting Scholar
University of California at Los Angeles

THE AUTHOR

Jack Carr was born in Toronto in 1944 and was graduated from the University of Toronto in 1965 before taking his PhD. at the University of Chicago in 1971. In 1968 he joined the department of Political Economy in the University of Toronto and became Associate Professor in 1973. Professor Carr is also a Research Associate of the Institute for Policy Analysis at the University of Toronto. During the 1975-76 academic year he is a Visiting Scholar at the Department of Economics, University of California in Los Angeles.

Professor Carr's publications include: *The Money Supply and the Rate of Inflation*, a study prepared for the Prices and Incomes Commission in 1972; *Cents and Nonsense* (Holt, Rinehart and Winston), a book of popular essays on economic policy, and numerous contributions to scholarly journals.

Wage and Price Controls
Panacea for Inflation
or
Prescription for Disaster?

JACK CARR

Associate Professor of Economics
University of Toronto
Visiting Scholar
University of California at Los Angeles

I. INTRODUCTION

On October 13, 1975 Prime Minister Trudeau addressed the Canadian public on national radio and television and announced the imposition of a comprehensive scheme of mandatory wage and price controls. The Prime Minister made it clear at that time that these controls were being imposed to attack the inflation problem in Canada. The use of wage and price controls by government to fight inflation is not a novel approach. The first recorded example of wage and price controls dates back to 301 A.D. At that time, the Roman Emperor Diocletian put a price ceiling on over 900 commodities, 130 different grades of labour and on a large number of freight rates.[1] Canada in the Second World War placed ceilings on a large number of prices and wages.[2] England and a number of European countries have imposed price and wage controls[3] at various times in the 50's, 60's and 70's.[4] More recently and closer to home the United States imposed wage and price controls starting August 1971 and ending April 1974.[5] In fact, the controls just adopted by Canada are very similar to Phase IV of the U.S. control system.

The current Canadian controls limit wage increases, in general, to the 8 per cent to 12 per cent range and allow prices charged by firms to increase only when the firm's costs increase. Prices are allowed to go up only enough to enable firms to recover their increased costs. In this way the controls attempt to freeze in dollar amounts profit per unit of output of firms.

This chapter will attempt to analyze the economic effects of the wage and price controls currently being placed on Canadians. Will these controls achieve their goal and reduce inflation in Canada? What is the price of these controls? Will these controls lead to shortages, inefficiencies in the operation of the Canadian economy, black markets, and perhaps even more controls? Before investigating these questions, there is one question that has to be looked at first. Since the controls are aimed at fighting inflation, before we can tell whether controls will succeed in their goal of reduced inflation, we have to understand what causes inflation in the first place. Let us now examine this question.

II. CAUSES OF INFLATION

What is inflation?

The word 'inflation' has acquired various meanings in recent years and as a consequence there is confusion over what economists mean when they talk about inflation. One hears about 'land price inflation', 'housing price inflation', 'food price inflation', 'oil price inflation' and so on. The traditional meaning of inflation[6] and *the meaning of inflation* that will be used in this paper is that inflation represents a general increase in the price of all goods and services. Economists refer to the price of all goods and services as the absolute price level. Hence inflation is the increase in the absolute price level. When oil prices or food prices increase at a faster rate than other prices this will not be referred to as 'oil price inflation' or 'food price inflation'. Instead, we will say the relative price of food or oil has increased. It is necessary to bear in mind the distinction between the absolute price level and relative prices. When economists talk about prices they do not always make it clear whether they are referring to the absolute price level or to relative prices.

Absolute and relative prices

This confusion between absolute and relative prices leads to confusion about the causes of inflation. The causes of relative price changes always lie in changes in the demand for, or supply of, the particular good or service in question. Oil prices have increased because the producers have formed a cartel and have restricted the supply of oil. It is this phenomenon which is responsible for oil prices increasing relative to the price of other goods. Bad harvests in the recent past have reduced the supply of agricultural commodities and caused the relative price of food to increase. These individual supply and demand factors are responsible for the fact that the price of one commodity has increased relative to the price of another commodity. They do not explain why the price of all commodities has been rising.

Table 1 — Percentage Change in
Consumer Price Index, Canada

Year	Percentage Change in Consumer Price Index*	Average Change for Period
1960	1.3	
1961	.2	
1962	1.6	1.4
1963	1.8	
1964	1.9	
1965	2.9	
1966	3.6	
1967	4.1	3.9
1968	4.1	
1969	4.6	
1970	1.5	1.5
1971	5.0	
1972	5.1	7.9
1973	9.1	
1974	12.4	
1975	10.4	

*The percentage change in the Consumer Price Index for any year is calculated as the percentage change between the Consumer Price Index of December of that year and the figure for December of the previous year.

Source: Statistics Canada: *Canadian Statistical Review.*

Measuring inflation

If inflation is the increase in the absolute price level, the next question to ask is how does one go about measuring this absolute price level? This problem has been considered for a long time and the conclusion is that there is really no ideal way to measure the absolute price level. The measure of the absolute price level that will be used in this paper is the Consumer Price Index (CPI) compiled and issued monthly by Statistics Canada. The Consumer Price Index is an average of prices of goods and services that the typical Canadian urban family purchases. The rate of inflation will be defined in this paper as the percentage change in the Consumer Price Index. Table 1 presents the rate of inflation in Canada during the last 15 years. The figures in Table 1 do not support the common belief that prices have steadily increased over the last 15 years. In fact one can divide the last 15 or so years into four distinct periods.

1. In the first part of the 1960's from 1960 to 1964 there was, for all practical purposes, no inflation.[7] The average inflation rate for that period was 1.4 per cent.

2. In the second half of the 1960's, from 1965 to 1969, the inflation rate increased to just under 4 per cent.

3. In 1970, inflation fell back drastically to 1.5 per cent.

4. From 1971 on, inflation has been high and seemingly increasing year by year.

For the past couple of years the Canadian economy has been experiencing double-digit inflation. In response to this high and accelerating inflation rate the government has imposed wage and price controls.

Questions about the causes

What factor or factors have been responsible for this pattern of inflation in Canada during the last fifteen years? It is possible to get many answers to this question since economists have substantial disagreements among themselves on the causes of inflation. It should be noted that this disagreement exists only with respect to relatively mild rates of inflation (say inflation rates under 20 per cent). For very high rates of inflation[8] practically all economists would look to excessive growth in the money supply[9] as the culprit. Because of this debate on the causes of inflation I will consider each theory in turn. For each theory I will first explore the theoretical arguments behind it and then see how well the theory explains the data for the Canadian economy over the last fifteen years. I firmly believe that only one of the explanations of inflation has a strong theoretical underpinning. In addition, this is the only theory that explains the data. I will present this theory at the end. Let me first present the theories that I consider to lack both theoretical underpinning and empirical confirmation.

1. Cost or price-push theories of inflation

This theory of inflation blames either greedy labour unions or greedy businessmen for the inflationary process. Inflation, according to this theory, starts *either* with a labour union negotiating arbitrarily high wages, causing firms to increase their prices, which in turn cause labour to ask for even higher wages and then the whole process is repeated again and again and again, *or* inflation starts with large business firms arbitrarily raising prices causing labour unions to seek higher wages which in turn cause the firms to raise prices even more. Then the whole process is repeated again and again and again. This theory has a number of supporters because it seems to appeal to common-sense and to the way the real world is actually run.

If you were to ask a Canadian businessman why is he raising his prices, he will invariably give you the same answer time and time again. He will explain to you that the prices of all his inputs are rising: the rental price of his office and factory space, the price of machinery and equipment, the price of new materials and the price of labour. The businessman will tell you he is raising his prices because his costs are increasing.

Wages the culprit?

In addition, it is likely the businessman will add that his major costs are wages (in Canadian manufacturing, labour costs represent about 70 per cent of total costs). Hence the major culprit in price increases is wage increases. It is not surprising, therefore, to find large numbers of businessmen who believe greedy workers (or more particularly greedy labour unions) to be the major cause of the inflationary process.

On the other side of the coin, if one were to ask a labour union leader why is he pushing for higher wages, invariably he will give you the same answer time and time again. He will explain to you that his is an elected position. If he doesn't do what the workers want, they will elect someone who will. He will go on to tell you that when workers spend their pay cheques they find the prices of practically all the commodities they buy have increased. The price of food, the price of clothing, the price of transportation, the price of housing accommodations have all increased. They need increased money wages just to maintain the same standard of living that they have been used to. Hence, labour groups blame the inflationary process on greedy businessmen who raise prices and start the wage-price spiral rolling.

Two flaws in the cost-push philosopher's stone

These arguments seem to make sense but have two fatal flaws. One flaw is a mistake that is often made in economics. This mistake is known as the *fallacy of composition*: what is true for the individual is not necessarily true for the community or economy as a whole. Consider the following example. Suppose you were in a crowd watching a parade. It is certainly true that if you were to stand on your toes you could see the parade better. It is not true that if everyone stood on his toes everyone watching the parade could see better. One can not generalize from the individual to the totality of individuals.

It is certainly true that individual businessmen raise their prices because costs increase. It is also certainly true that individual labour unions push for higher wages because the prices of the goods their members buy increase. But what is true for individual businessmen and labour unions does not represent 'true' causes of inflation for the economy as a whole. Inflation is an increase in all prices, the prices of final goods and services and the prices of factors of production (e.g. the price of labour). It makes no sense to take one subset of these prices and argue that increases in these prices are causing the rest of the prices to increase. To explain inflation one has to explain why all the prices are increasing.

The other flaw in the cost or price-push inflation argument is the theory on which it is based. The theory starts with either big business or big labour arbitrarily raising prices or wages. The theory argues that big business (and by big business they mean firms with monopoly power) or big labour (and again big labour means labour unions with monopoly power) have some discretion in the setting of the prices of the goods and services they sell. It is this discretionary power, it is argued, that allows these groups to arbitrarily raise prices. It is further argued that firms or workers in a competitive environment have no discretionary power in setting prices. They receive whatever prices prevail in the market. They are price takers rather than price makers. Hence it is concluded that it is the existence of monopoly power which is responsible for cost or price-push inflation.

Monopoly power the problem?

Let us consider the argument that monopoly power results in cost or price-push inflation. Price theory tells us that a monopolist (or any other economic actor) will be as greedy as he possibly can. He will attempt to obtain as great a profit as he can. Under most circumstances there is a unique price that will maximize the profits of a monopolist. If a price higher than this is charged, sales will fall off causing revenues to decline at a faster rate than costs decline and hence causing a decline in profits. Let us assume there is a greedy monopolist who is charging a price that maximizes his profit. What discretionary power does he have? If he changes price in any direction, profits will fall off. If nothing else changes, our greedy 'friend' will not change his price. Similarly, labour unions enjoying government-sanctioned monopoly power will not arbitrarily raise wages.† To do so would be against their best interest.

It is possible to make a case for monopolists of either kind raising prices. If for some reason they didn't charge the monopoly price in the previous period it would make sense to raise prices in the current period. This argument isn't too appealing since it implies that a rather 'stupid' monopolist suddenly wakes up to the fact that he has unused market power and begins to use it. Another possibility is that the extent of monopoly power (in either the business or labour sector) increases. This will cause profit maximizing monopolists to raise their prices. Even this argument can not explain inflation in the economy as a whole. Increasing monopoly power will result in higher relative prices in the monopolized sector of the economy. These higher prices result from reductions in the supply of the monopolized product. The monopolized firms will thus employ fewer resources. These resources will flow to other industries causing wages and prices to fall there. There will be no general inflation. The existence of monopoly power (or increasing monopoly power) affects relative prices but not the absolute price level. What is true about monopoly power is that monopolists restrict supply and cause a higher price to prevail in the market than would be the case if the market were competitively organized. Monopoly power can be responsible for a higher relative price in the monopolized sector; it is not responsible for higher rates of increase in prices in the monopolized sector.

Does greed explain inflation?

It can be seen that there is no theoretical support for cost or price-push inflation. Is there any empirical support for this view of inflation? Let us go back to Table 1 and consider in-

---

†Editor's Note: Strictly speaking, monopoly situations in either labour or commodities can only arise to the extent that government provides the monopolist with the exclusive right to supply the commodity or service. Monopoly market power is effectively implemented by control over the supply of the commodity or service. For example, in the case of unions, the 'closed shop' provision gives the union exclusive power over the supply of labour services to unionized firms. Given the need that firms have for labour services, unions can control wages by changing the supply of labour services.

flation rates in Canada for the last 15 years. Can one use cost or price-push inflation to explain this pattern of inflation?

From 1960 to 1964 where were the greedy businessmen and greedy labour union leaders? Did they just learn to be greedy in 1965? Were they unaware from 1960 to 1964 and suddenly realized their monopoly power in 1965? Did they lose their greed again in 1970? All this seems highly unlikely. What one realizes immediately is that cost-push or price-push theories can not explain periods of stable prices. This theory can not explain periods of deflation. In the Great Depression in Canada the price level fell significantly from 1929 to 1933. Where were the greedy businessmen and greedy labour union leaders then? As can be seen, the existence of monopoly power can not explain the price inflation behaviour in Canada of the last 15 years. Studies by the Prices and Incomes Commission in Canada[10] and Philip Cagan[11] in the United States failed to find a relationship between the pattern of price change and monopoly power that is predicted by cost or price-push theories.

Consider the sophisticated version of cost and price-push theories. This version contends that increasing monopoly power of business and labour unions causes inflation. For this to explain Canada's recent experience with inflation, monopoly power had to be increasing from 1965 to 1969, fall drastically in 1970 and then steadily rise from 1971 on. Although measures of monopoly power are difficult to come by, it is highly unlikely that monopoly power could fluctuate enough to explain periods of deflation, periods of stable prices and periods of inflation.

On the basis of the above discussion one would have to conclude that there is no theoretical or empirical basis for a belief in cost or price-push theories of inflation.[12]

2. Sociological theories of inflation

Sociological theories of inflation are very similar to cost or price-push theories. They make no pretense of having any theoretical foundations whatever. They blame inflation on the greed of economic units. They argue that inflation is the result of everyone trying to obtain a bigger share of the income pie. Since it is impossible for everyone to get a bigger share, inflation results. These theories do not consider how prices and wages are determined in a market economy. They merely state that inconsistent demands of various groups in the economy result in inflation. These theories can blame almost anyone and everyone for inflation.

Since they do not blame the government for inflation, many governments espouse these theories. For example, it would appear that the present Canadian government believes in this theory. In Prime Minister Trudeau's address to the nation explaining the imposition of wage and price controls he stated that

> "the basic cause of inflation in Canada is the attempt by too many people and too many groups to increase their money incomes at rates faster than the increase in the nation's wealth".[13]

The problem with the sociological theories of inflation is that they seem only to explain those periods in history characterized by rising inflation. No one invokes these sorts of theories to explain slow downs in the economy or even periods of relative stability. Perhaps the reason these theories are not used to explain deflation — falling prices or prices growing more slowly — is that the explanation is fundamentally implausible.

If we use this theory to attempt to explain the last fifteen years of Canada's inflation record we find ourselves asserting what seem to be absurd sorts of behaviour. For example, we might find ourselves saying the following sorts of things: from 1960 to 1964 inflation grew at a modest rate — less than two per cent — owing to the fact that Canadian greed on average, grew at the modest rate of 5 or 6 per cent per year (the average rate at which the income pie grew). However, greed took a nasty turn in the 1965 to 1969 period as greedy workers and greedy capitalists fought for a limited income pie and as a result the inflation rate — reflecting the increased greed — rose to 4.1 per cent. 1970 was, however, a year of brotherly love and saw the inflation rate fall back to the two per cent range. 1970 proved a brief respite in the greed surge, however, and currently the inflation rate, fueled by a seemingly unlimited growth in greed, is at record levels.

It is truly difficult to have much confidence in a theory that asserts that a characteristic of a population such as greed could be so changeable from one year to the next. It simply is not plausible that people would be very greedy one year and not at all greedy during the next year only to change again in the following year. Apart from this basic implausibility, greed is not capable of explaining an increase in all prices as was demonstrated in the preceeding section.

The cause for inflation, it seems, is not likely to be found in a 'witch-hunt' for greedy people. The greed theory doesn't seem to explain past rates of inflation.

3. Phillips Curve theory of inflation

In the 1930's and 1940's, economists devoted most of their attention to the unemployment problem and hardly considered the problem of inflation at all. One reason for this is that many economists believed that as long as there was unemployment, inflation could not exist.[14] In the 50's and 60's, inflation existed in a number of countries with substantial unemployment. Economists then turned to the task of explaining the co-existence of inflation and unemployment. The relationship between inflation and unemployment became known as the Phillips Curve.[15]

The relationship between inflation and unemployment was explained by Phillips in the following economic argument. When unemployment was very high, unemployed workers would compete for jobs and bid wage rates down. When unemployment was very low, firms would compete in their search for workers and bid wages up. It was argued that the percentage change in the wage rate was negatively related to the unemployment rate. The lower the unemployment rate the higher would be the percentage increase in wages. It is then argued that when wage rates are bid up, firms will have higher costs and will increase prices. Hence, the lower the unemployment rate the higher would be the percentage increase in wages and the higher would be the percentage increase in prices.

The trade-off

The Phillips Curve seemed not only to explain the *co-existence* of inflation and unemployment but also the *trade-off* between inflation and unemployment. This theory claimed that the only way an economy could move to a position of lower inflation would be to accept a position of higher unemployment. The Phillips Curve hypothesis argues that a proximate cause of inflation is unemployment. A lower rate of unemployment implies a higher rate of wage and, ultimately, price inflation.

Fooling all the people all the time

This theory seems to make a lot of sense but it too has one fatal flaw. The theory assumes that workers care about the dollar amount of their wages (i.e., the number of one dollar bills they receive in exchange for their labour) rather than the amount of goods and services that their wages can purchase (i.e., their real wages). If money wages double and the prices of all goods and services double, would anyone expect workers to supply more labour? The answer should be that when, and it may take some time, workers fully realize that all prices have doubled[16] they will recognize the fact that they are not any better off with their higher money wages. Hence, they will not accept new offers of employment and hence the unemployment rate will not fall when the inflation rate increases. People are not long fooled by higher money wages especially in inflationary climates (i.e., workers do not suffer from money illusion).†

There is no theoretical support, apart from assuming that workers are easily fooled and suffer from money illusion, for a stable lasting relationship between the inflation rate and the rate of unemployment. (In a subsequent section I explore the notion of a temporary relationship of this form.) A Phillips Curve type relationship could be derived between percentage changes in the real wage rate (where the real wage rate is defined as money wages deflated by the absolute price level) and the unemployment rate. But the theory would tell us nothing about inflation. A knowledge of what is happening to real wages in no way enables one to predict what is happening to the inflation rate.

---

†Editor's Note: In short, as Abraham Lincoln said, "You (politicians) may fool all of the people some of the time, (*periods of inflation*); you (politicians) can even fool some of the people all the time (*unfortunately*); but you (*politicians*) can't fool all of the people all of the time" (*sustained inflation*).

Confronting the Phillips Curve

Let us now see if Canadian experience (presented in table 2) of the last fifteen years conforms to a Phillips Curve explanation. From 1961 to 1966 unemployment rates steadily

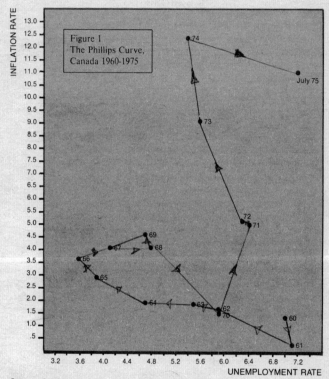

Figure I
The Phillips Curve,
Canada 1960-1975

Source: Statistics Canada, *Canadian Statistical Review*

fell in Canada and the inflation rate exhibited a gradual rising pattern over this period. These years agree with the traditional Phillips Curve pattern. From 1967 to 1972 unemployment rates exhibited a rising trend but so did inflation rates. From 1973 to mid-1975 once again rising unemployment was accompanied by rising inflation. The

Table 2 — Inflation and Unemployment Rates,
Canada 1960-1975

Year	Percentage Change in Consumer Price Index	Unemployment Rate
1960	1.3	7.0
1961	.2	7.1
1962	1.6	5.9
1963	1.8	5.5
1964	1.9	4.7
1965	2.9	3.9
1966	3.6	3.6
1967	4.1	4.1
1968	4.1	4.8
1969	4.6	4.7
1970	1.5	5.9
1971	5.0	6.4
1972	5.1	6.3
1973	9.1	5.6
1974	12.4	5.4
July 1974-July 1975	11.0	7.2 (July 1975)

Source: Statistics Canada: *Canadian Statistical Review.*

Canadian experience clearly rejects the notion that there exists any simple Phillips Curve and any stable trade-off between inflation and unemployment. It would appear that the Phillips Curve is not a fruitful place to look for the cause of inflation.

4. Expectations theory of inflation

There are those who argue that 'expectations' of inflation are the main cause of inflation. It is claimed that if only people didn't expect inflation then inflation would disappear by itself. The problem with this theory is that it doesn't explain why people all of a sudden started to expect inflation in the mid 1960's. The answer is that people expect inflation when there is inflation. Expectations of inflation are an effect of the inflationary phenomenon, not a cause. When inflation ends, inflationary expectations disappear.

5. Profiteering theory of inflation

Since the time of Diocletian, nearly 1700 years ago, inflation has been blamed on profiteers and speculators. In a way, this theory is similar to price-push inflation. But rather than blaming producers of goods and services for the inflation, this theory tends to blame greedy middlemen who buy goods at a 'low' price and sell them at a 'high' price without in any way altering the basic character of the goods.[17] The same criticisms against price-push inflation apply here. Middlemen may be responsible for higher relative prices of the commodities in which they deal but there are no theoretical arguments that they are responsible for a higher rate of increase in the prices of commodities. In a practical vein, is a period of price stability to be explained by a fall in the greed of middlemen? It appears that one cannot look to greedy middlemen for the cause of inflation.

6. Monetary theory of inflation[18]

Up to now we have rejected on theoretical grounds and on the basis of a casual review of the facts, five theories of inflation. Let us now consider a theory that has strong theoretical underpinnings and even stronger empirical support. The monetary theory of inflation argues that inflation is at all times and in all places a monetary phenomenon. This theory is not a new theory; it has certainly stood the test of time. It is at least 500 years old. It was first used to explain the inflation Spain experienced in the sixteenth century after the Spanish conquerors brought substantial amounts of gold back from the Americas. It is the theory that most economists advocate to explain periods of very rapid price rise or hyperinflation. I will argue that this theory, which explains periods of rapid inflation, also explains periods of mild inflation.

What the theory says

The monetary theory of inflation argues that when the money supply is increased at a rate faster than the rate of growth of real output in the economy then inflation will occur. The inflation rate may be approximated in the first instance by the rate of growth of the money supply minus the rate of growth of output. The term 'approximated' is used above for a number of reasons. In the short-run, other factors (such as fiscal policy) may temporarily affect the inflation rate. In addition, as in most economic relationships, there are lags between the time when the money supply (or its rate of growth) changes and when the absolute price level (or the inflation rate) changes. These lags can be as short as a few months or as long as a couple of years.[19] Also, high rates of inflation set up a predictable chain of forces which alters the relationship between money supply growth and the inflation rate. With these provisos aside, the monetary theory of inflation argues that substantial increases in the rate of growth of the money supply always lead to substantial increases in the inflation rate and that inflation will never end unless the excessive growth in the money supply is stopped. It will be noted that this theory is capable of explaining periods of stable prices and even periods of deflation.

Too many dollars

The basic logic behind this theory is that money performs a service for the people who hold it. Money facilitates exchange; that is, as compared to a barter situation, money reduces the nuisance costs involved in buying and selling. Because of the services that money yields, individuals in the economy maintain money balances. The amount of money balances individuals desire to hold is determined by several factors — principally the individual's income. In the Canadian economy in mid-1975 Canadians, according to the Bank of Canada, were on average holding money balances (including savings deposits) equivalent to about 19 weeks of income. This means an individual making $100 per week would have in cash on hand and deposits in the bank about $1900.

To illustrate how this theory works imagine, for simplicity, an economy where the output of goods and services is fixed (i.e., output is not growing).† Let us further imagine the situation in this economy if the government were to print more money and give it in equal amounts to every Canadian as, say, a Good Canadian Award. In-

---

†Editor's Note: The Canadian economy during the first half of 1975 closely resembled this case — output of goods and services fell slightly.

dividuals in the economy would soon find that they were holding money balances in excess of their desired holdings (e.g., our individual earning $100 per week might be holding $2100 in money balances — 21 weeks of income in money balances rather than the desired level of 19 weeks of income in money balances). What will people do with excess money balances?† The monetary theory of inflation argues that people will not put these excess money balances under their mattresses. Ultimately, individuals will attempt to spend these excess cash balances on goods and services.

Everyone in the economy has excess cash balances and everyone is attempting to increase his purchases. But we have supposed that the quantity of real output is fixed. Everyone can not obtain more goods and services. Everyone attempting to do so will merely drive all prices up. Hence an increase in the money supply with the quantity of output fixed leads to an increase in the absolute price level. One can easily modify the above example for the case of a growing economy. In such a case if the money supply increases at a faster rate than output is increasing, inflation results.

The above represents a brief and simplified summary of the monetary theory of inflation. To arrive at its conclusions the monetary theory of inflation did not have to assume that individuals in the economy were either stupid, easily fooled, irrational or suffering from money illusion. The monetary theory of inflation is derived using the traditional tools of economics.

Theory applied - four Canadian episodes

Table 3 presents figures for the rate of growth of the money supply, rate of inflation and rate of growth of real output for the last 15 years in Canada. To put these figures in proper historical perspective it should be noted that from 1926 to 1966 the rate of growth of the money supply in Canada averaged about 6 per cent per year, the rate of growth of real

---

†Editor's Note: Of course, people may decide to simply keep the excess cash. In the same vein, people may, for some reason, decide that they should keep 14 or 22 weeks of income in the form of cash or deposits. The theory being discussed here does not preclude these possibilities. It says, rather, that there is a strong element of habit built into people's behaviour and that people's attitude toward their cash holdings is unlikely to change unless there is a change in their basic economic circumstances.

Table 3 — Inflation, Money Supply Growth and
Rate of Growth of Real Output, Canada 1960-1975

Year	Percentage Change in Consumer Price Index	Average for Period	Percentage Change in Money Supply*	Average for Period	Rate of Growth of Real Output	Average for Period
1960	1.3		4.6		2.9	
1961	.2		8.6		2.9	
1962	1.6		3.8	6.2	6.8	4.9
1963	1.8	1.7	6.4		5.2	
1964	1.9		7.4		6.7	
1965	2.9		12.0		6.7	
1966	3.6		6.5	11.9	6.9	5.7
1967	4.1	4.1	15.9		3.3	
1968	4.1		13.3		5.8	
1969	4.6		3.9		5.3	
1970	1.5		10.8		2.6	
1971	5.0		14.9	15.0	5.8	
1972	5.1	7.9	15.9		5.8	5.3
1973	9.1		18.3		6.9	
1974	12.4		16.8		2.8	
July, 1974- July, 1975	11.0		17.1		-1.3†	

*Money supply is defined as the sum of currency in circulation outside banks plus all Canadian dollar deposits privately held.
†Output growth rate is for second quarter 1975 over second quarter 1974.

Source: Statistics Canada: *Canadian Statistical Review.*

output averaged about 4 per cent per year and the rate of increase of prices averaged about 2 per cent per year.[20] The first thing to note is that for this long period in Canadian history the monetary theory of inflation provided a fairly accurate prediction of the inflation rate. Previously it was argued that the monetary theory of inflation is not a mechanical formula for predicting inflation. In the short-run, the inflation rate will not exactly equal the rate of growth of the money supply minus the rate of growth of output. For this reason let us look at sub-periods of the last 15 years in Canada and see what was happening to money and prices. In looking at the last 15 years we can find four sub-periods each with a distinct monetary policy.

Sub-period one

From 1960 to 1964, the money supply grew at an average rate of 6.2 per cent per year. This figure is approximately equal to the long-term average growth in the money supply (i.e. the average growth rate in money from 1926 to 1966). One can label this period as one of moderate monetary expansion. With moderate monetary expansion in the early 60's the Canadian economy experienced a moderate increase in the price level in that same period.[21] From 1961 to 1965 the inflation rate averaged 1.7 per cent. With moderate monetary expansion, Canada experienced practically no inflation. However, this moderate policy turned out to be short-lived.

Sub-period two

In the latter part of the 1960's monetary policy took a sharp swing upward. From 1965 to 1968 the Canadian government was following an expansionary monetary policy allowing the money supply to grow on average 11.9 per cent per year. The monetary theory of inflation would predict that this expansionary monetary policy would lead to inflation. This is exactly what happened. From 1966 to 1969 the inflation rate averaged 4.1 per cent. Increases in the rate of growth of the money supply led to increases in the inflation rate.

Sub-period three

At the beginning of 1969 the Canadian government started to get worried about the economic consequences of inflation and decided to do something about it. From March 1968 to March 1969 money supply growth reached a peak rate of growth of 17.1 per cent. From March 1969 to March 1970 there was a complete turnaround in monetary policy. During this period the money supply grew only 0.3 per cent per annum. This contractionary monetary policy led to a fall in the inflation rate (and in addition to the recession of 1970).[22]

Sub-period four

From April 1970 to the present, Canada has experienced very high rates of growth of the money supply. Money supply growth reached a peak in excess of 18 per cent per year and averaged about 15 per cent per annum for the first four years of the 1970's. This figure should be compared to the 6 per cent long-term average growth rate in the money supply. High growth rates in the money supply inevitably led to high rates of inflation. From 1971 to 1974 inflation averaged 7.4 per cent per year and reached into double-digits in the last part of this period.

The last fifteen years of Canadian experience have (unfortunately) provided a very good set of 'experiments' to test the monetary theory of inflation. *With moderate monetary growth there was no inflation in Canada. With expansionary monetary growth there was relatively mild inflation. When the monetary growth rate fell, the inflation rate fell. When monetary growth rates reached into the sky, Canada experienced double-digit inflation.*

At the end of the period of moderate monetary expansion in 1964 the money supply was growing at 7.4 per cent per annum and prices were increasing at 1.9 per cent. By mid-1975 money supply growth had increased by 9.7 percentage points and the inflation rate had increased by 9.1 per-

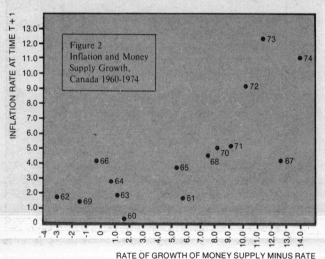

Figure 2
Inflation and Money
Supply Growth,
Canada 1960-1974

Source: Statistics Canada, *Canadian Statistical Review*

centage points. These last 15 years of data are consistent with the monetary theory of inflation. This is the only theory up to now which can adequately explain this period in Canadian history.

Although it is not as meaningful to look at year by year changes, Figure 2 plots for Canada values for the rate of growth of the money supply minus the rate of growth of output against the rate of inflation for the following year. It can be seen from this chart that, in general, as money supply growth increases, inflation increases. Empirical support for the monetary theory of inflation not only exists for Canada over the last 15 and the last 50 years, support also exists for this theory using the data from a large number of countries.

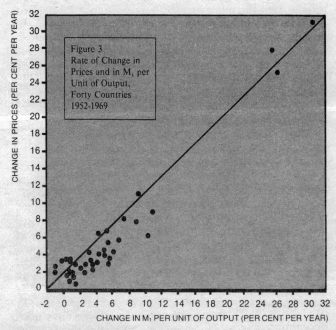

Figure 3
Rate of Change in
Prices and in M₁ per
Unit of Output,
Forty Countries
1952-1969

Source: Anna Schwartz, "Secular Price Change in Historical Perspective," *Journal of Money, Credit and Banking*, February 1973.

Global evidence

Anna Schwartz[23] has examined the rate of growth of money in excess of the rate of growth of output for the period 1952 to 1969 in 40 countries and has compared these figures to the rates of inflation in these countries. Anna Schwartz's data are plotted in Figure 3. Again, one can see how closely these data conform to the monetary theory of inflation. With this evidence it is not hard to see how an economist like Milton Friedman concludes that "inflation is always and everywhere a monetary phenomenon."[24]

Why increase the money supply?

The monetary theory of inflation identifies the money supply as the proximate cause of inflation. It does not concern itself with the reasons why the Federal government manipulates the money supply in the way it does.[25] In looking at recent Canadian experience it is natural to ask the question why the government increased the rate of growth of the money supply in the mid-1960's? Previous to that Canada followed a sensible, moderate monetary policy. To understand the answer to the above question one has to understand the nature of international linkages under which Canada operates and the nature of the fixed exchange rate regime which existed in Canada from 1962 to mid-1970.

The crucial role of U.S. dollars

Foreign trade is very important to Canada. Exports (spending by foreigners on Canadian goods and services) generally account for about 25 per cent of total spending (or Gross National Expenditure) in Canada. The United States of America is Canada's largest trading partner. About 70 per cent of Canadian exports go to the United States. What was happening in the United States in the 1960's? In the mid-1960's the rate of growth of the money supply started to increase in the United States. (One can ask the question why the U.S. money supply started to increase. One contributing factor may have been America's increasing involvement in the Vietnam War. Historically, wartime expenditures have been financed by the government printing money. It is for this reason that wars are associated with inflationary periods.) The increase in the U.S. money supply resulted in inflation in the U.S. economy. U.S. inflation increased relative to Canadian inflation. With prices rising faster in the U.S. than in Canada, Americans found Canadian goods more attractive and Canadians found U.S. goods less attractive. This tended to increase Canadian exports to the U.S. and decrease Canadian imports from the U.S. — a trade pattern which had implications for the Canadian money supply.

Whenever Canadians export to the U.S. they earn a supply of foreign exchange (i.e. U.S. dollars) and whenever they import from the U.S. they use up foreign exchange. Rising Canadian exports and falling Canadian imports imply an increase in the supply of foreign exchange and a decrease in the demand for foreign exchange. With the price of foreign exchange (i.e. the exchange rate) staying constant there will be an excess supply of foreign exchange. In free markets when excess supplies exist the price will fall to restore a balance in supply and demand. The price in the exchange market could not adjust in the 1960's since Canada was on a system of fixed exchange rates. For Canada this meant that the Canadian government was responsible for maintaining a fixed price of the U.S. dollar in terms of the Canadian dollar.

Imported inflation?

To maintain the fixed price of the U.S. dollar, the Canadian government in the mid-1960's was forced to purchase the excess supply of U.S. dollars. The Canadian government purchased these U.S. dollars with newly-printed Canadian dollars. Hence the Canadian government was forced to increase monetary expansion. One of the lessons of fixed exchange rates is that under them a country can not run an independent monetary policy. Canada should not blame the inflation of the late 1960's on the U.S. but on the nature of the exchange rate system. Canada could have avoided increasing monetary expansion if it had chosen a system of floating exchange rates (i.e. a system where the price of foreign exchange adjusts whenever there is excess supply or demand rather than a system where the government intervenes to prevent price movements).

Biting the bullet

In 1969 the Trudeau government desired to end inflation. *At that time the government knew where the blame for inflation lay.* It didn't stop greedy businessmen or greedy labour unions from acting in their own self- interest. *It stopped the printing presses* instead. Such action is very difficult under a fixed exchange rate regime. In April and May of 1970 the money supply in Canada grew at very large rates. I believe it was the desire to maintain a policy of 'tight' money[26] that convinced the government to abandon fixed exchange rates and adopt a system of floating exchange rates. The irony of the situation is that Canada adopted floating exchange rates in order to maintain a policy of minimal monetary growth. However, the resulting recession in 1970 was more severe than the government had expected. It seems that because of this, Canadian monetary policy turned around again in 1970. Since mid-1970 the money supply has been growing at very high annual rates; rates inconsistent with price stability; rates consistent with double- digit inflation.

Once burnt

One postscript should be added to this story of Canadian monetary policy. It has significance in answering the question why a reduction in monetary growth was not used to fight inflation in 1975 but instead comprehensive wage and price controls were imposed on the economy. In 1972 the Trudeau government fought an election and almost lost. The Liberals lost their parliamentary majority and received the smallest of pluralities. It seems that this Liberal near-defeat was interpreted by the Trudeau government as a repudiation of its 'tight' money policy of 1969 which resulted in high unemployment in 1970. It seems the government has learned its lesson. From its actions it would appear that the Trudeau government has foresworn the only effective tool in fighting inflation, i.e. reducing monetary growth. It would appear that the Trudeau government views that the political costs of reducing monetary growth are too high to warrant such action.

World-wide excess

The story that has been told of Canada in the last half of the 1960's could be told again and again for countries such as France, Germany, Japan and many others. With rising U.S. inflation rates in the 1960's these countries exported more to the U.S. and imported less from the U.S. They all faced excess supplies of U.S. dollars. They all were on a fixed exchange rate system. France bought up their excess supplies of U.S. dollars with newly-printed francs. Germany bought up U.S. dollars in exchange for newly-printed marks. The same sequence of events caused the Japanese to print more yen. The nature of the fixed exchange rate regime forced increases in money supplies in response to the U.S. increase in its money supply. This resulted in world-wide inflation. The monetary theory of inflation is not only capable of explaining inflation in Canada but it also explains the world-wide inflation of the late 1960's and early 1970's.

7. Government expenditure theory of inflation

It is sometimes argued that whenever government expenditures exceed government revenues this puts inflationary pressure on the economy. In one sense this theory can be viewed as a refinement of the monetary theory of inflation. Government expenditures can be financed in one of three ways: from tax revenues, from borrowing from the public (i.e. issuing government bonds) or by 'printing' money.[27] If government expenditures in excess of revenues are financed through money issue then inflationary pressure will result. The theory viewed in this way becomes an adjunct to the monetary theory. It answers the question why the money supply increases when it does.

There are those who argue that government deficits (i.e. expenditures in excess of revenues) no matter how financed will result in inflation. They argue that continual government deficits result in permanent inflation. The theory behind this argument lies in the proposition that government expenditures on goods and services add to the overall demand pressures in the economy. This increase in aggregate demand results in an increase in the price level. There would be no quarrelling with this argument in the case where deficits were financed by money issue. However, consider the case where deficits are financed by government borrowing. When the government borrows from the private sector, the ability of the private sector to maintain its level of consumption has correspondingly been reduced. Government demand has gone up and private demand has decreased. There is no reason why total demand need increase and why the price level should rise.[28]

Table 4 presents recent inflation rates and levels of balance in Canada's Federal government budget. A casual look at the table will show that inflationary periods have existed with both government surpluses, and government deficits. Looking at figure 4 will also convince one that money supply growth is not determined solely by the level of government deficits or surpluses. Periods of surplus have existed with

Table 4 — Inflation and Federal Government Surplus or Deficit, Canada 1960-1975

Year	Percentage Change in Consumer Price Index	Federal Government Surplus (+) or Deficit (-)[a]
1960	1.3	-.229
1961	.2	-.410
1962	1.6	-.507
1963	1.8	-.285
1964	1.9	.337
1965	2.9	.551
1966	3.6	.294
1967	4.1	-.085
1968	4.1	-.033
1969	4.6	1.021
1970	1.5	.264
1971	5.0	-.095
1972	5.1	-.701
1973	9.1	.222
1974	12.4	.593
July 1974-July 1975	11.0	-5.265 [b]

a) Surplus or deficit is measured on a national accounts basis in billions of dollars.
b) Second quarter figures seasonally adjusted at annual rates.

Source: Statistics Canada: *Canadian Statistical Review.*

high rates of growth of the money supply. The evidence would seem to indicate that the state of the government balance alone is not capable of explaining inflation in Canada over the last 15 years.†

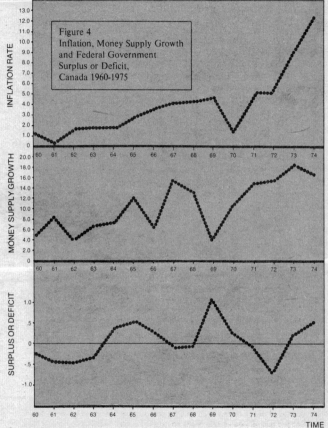

Figure 4
Inflation, Money Supply Growth
and Federal Government
Surplus or Deficit,
Canada 1960-1975

Source: Statistics Canada, *Canadian Statistical Review*

†Editor's Note: The correlation between the money supply (and hence the inflation rate) and the government deficit measured on a cash requirement basis would be much closer than this analysis suggests. The cash requirement is probably a more meaningful measure of deficit since it includes all expenditures and revenues of the federal government.

Labelling the theories

Before leaving the subject of inflation one postscript should be added. Most textbooks in economics distinguish between two types of inflation: demand-pull and cost-push. This distinction has not been made here since not only do I not view this as a useful dichotomy but also I think it leads to much confusion on the subject matter of inflation. I believe there is only one type of inflation. Inflation is anywhere and everywhere the same disease. Inflation is anywhere and everywhere the result of the same cause: an excessive growth in the money supply.

For those accustomed to thinking in terms of demand-pull and cost-push let me try to apply these labels, where appropriate, to some of the theories discussed here. The monetary theory of inflation and the government expenditure theory may both be classified as demand-pull. They both concern themselves in some sense with an excess of aggregate demand over aggregate supply. The Phillips Curve explanation may be considered as a cross between demand-pull and cost-push. It contains elements from both theories. One can either view the unemployment rate as a proxy for the level of excess aggregate demand in the economy or one can view the unemployment rate as some crude measure of monopoly power of labour unions. The other theories discussed here do not fit into the nice neat categories of demand-pull or cost-push.

The main proposition that arises from the discussion in this section of the paper is that inflation is always and everywhere a monetary phenomenon.

III. INFLATION AND WAGE AND PRICE CONTROLS

In the previous section we concluded that there was no basis for the belief that greed in general, or greed in particular on the part of business or greed on the part of labour, had anything whatever to do with the problem of inflation. It was concluded that inflation was caused by excessive growth in the money supply. This being the case one can immediately see that wage and price controls do nothing to combat the basic cause of inflation.[29] Wage and price controls attack the symptoms of inflation without doing anything about its basic cause. The arguments advanced to support the position that wage and price controls reduce inflation depend crucially on the existence of cost or price-push inflation. Since there is no support for these theories of inflation there is no theoretical support for the proposition that wage and price controls will reduce the true rate of inflation.[30]

Two studies in this series examine the operation of economies under wage and price controls. Michael Darby in examining the U.S. economy in the 1970's under wage and price controls concludes that "the major direct effect of the Economic Stabilization Program (ESP) was to impart a significant bias to price indices such as the average price of total National Expenditure. . . When the data are corrected for quality changes, only Freeze I was successful at the stated goal of reducing the rate of inflation. Even that success was balanced by more rapid inflation in the next few quarters. The growth of the price level from the last pre-ESP quarter to the latest post-ESP quarter was certainly no less rapid than would have been anticipated in the program's absence."[31] Darby finds no evidence that wage and price controls in the U.S. reduced the inflation rate for the period 1971 to 1975. Michael Parkin in examining the British experience with controls concludes that "whatever their superficial attractiveness, they simply do not work. They do not control inflation".[32] This view is consistent with an earlier study of Lipsey and Parkin where they concluded that for Britain ". . . the data are not inconsistent with the view that wage and price restraints have usually been ineffective in restraining inflation. . ."[33]

There is no theoretical basis for the belief that wage and price controls reduce the inflation rate and all recent experiences with controls seem to confirm this theoretical conclusion.

An argument for controls

If wage and price controls don't reduce the inflation rate why then are they enacted? The arguments in support of U.S. controls were not based on the premise that controls would reduce inflation. Similarly, when the Prices and Incomes Commission in Canada recommended, in 1972, compulsory wage and price controls they did not do so because they believed controls would reduce inflation. The Prices and Incomes Commission specifically disavowed cost or price-push inflation, the one possible theory capable of supporting the proposition that controls reduce inflation.

"The Commission's view that a temporary program of direct controls over prices, wages and other incomes could be helpful in certain circumstances does not arise from a belief that the root of the inflation-unemployment dilemma lies in the ability of powerful unions and corporations to continue to push up costs and prices regardless of demand conditions".[34]

The Commission gave a novel and rather sophisticated argument for the implementation of controls.

The Commission discussed inflation in terms of excess aggregate demand without ever addressing the question of the source of this excess aggregate demand. Without altering any of the substantive points of the Commission's arguments we will talk in terms of excessive monetary growth as being the source of the excess aggregate demand. The argument then proceeds as follows. To illustrate the argument consider an economy where the money supply is growing at 15 per cent per year, output is growing at 5 per cent per year and the rate of inflation is 10 per cent per year. In addition, suppose this economy has experienced 10 per cent inflation for quite a long period of time. As a consequence everyone expects an inflation rate of 10 per cent. These expectations of inflation are built into all contracts negotiated in this economy.

In any economy, inflation can only be reduced if the rate of growth of the money supply is reduced. Suppose that in our hypothetical economy the growth in the money supply is unexpectedly reduced to 10 per cent per year. Initially the reduction in monetary growth will not lead to a reduction in the inflation rate. In any economy there are some prices and wages which are negotiated on a basis of long-term contracts. These prices and wages will be slow to adjust. Also, wages and prices will be set on the basis of expectations of inflation of 10 per cent. In the short-run, wages and prices will be rigid (i.e. will be little affected by changes in monetary growth). Consequently, a reduction in monetary growth will lead to a reduction in the rate of real economic activity.

Firms will find that sales are falling short of their expected level and hence they will reduce their rate of output. This in turn will cause the demand for labour to decrease. If wage rates were perfectly flexible, the lower demand for labour would cause lower wage rates. In the short-run wages are not flexible and the reduced demand for labour results in less workers being employed (i.e. results in unemployment). Wages are inflexible in the short-run for the same reason that prices of final products are inflexible. Some wages can not adjust in the short-run since they are negotiated on the basis of one or two year contracts. In addition, workers in setting and negotiating their wage demands assume a 10 per cent inflation rate. With the new lower demand for labour in the economy, wage demands by workers, incorporating a 10 per cent premium for expected inflation, will prove too high for all workers to find employment. As a consequence, unemployment will result.[35]

This unemployment is, however, only temporary. Eventually old contracts expire and new prices and wages will be negotiated and these new prices and wages will be more in line with the new, reduced rate of monetary growth in the economy. Since expectations about future inflation are based largely on the current and past behaviour of inflation in the economy, as the inflation rate falls, gradually expectations of inflation will also fall. With a fall in expectations of inflation, wage demands of workers will be reduced and more workers will find employment. Unemployment will fall. Full employment will occur when expectations of inflation are revised down to the equilibrium inflation rate of 5 per cent. One factor which influences the extent and duration of the temporary unemployment is the rate at which expectations of inflation are revised. The faster expectations of inflation are revised, the quicker will wage demands be revised and the less will be the temporary unemployment.

In the short-run, reducing the rate of growth of the money supply results in an increase in the unemployment rate. In the long-run, there is no relationship between inflation and unemployment. (Another way of phrasing this is to say there is a short-run Phillips Curve but no long-run Phillips Curve). These results could be seen very clearly in the performance of the Canadian economy in the late 1960's. We have already seen that from March 1968 to March 1969 the money supply grew at 17.1 per cent. From March 1969 to March 1970 there was a sudden turnaround and the money supply grew at 0.3 per cent. This sudden reduction in monetary growth was responsible for the recession of 1970. Unemployment increased and the rate of growth of output fell. This recession was relatively short-lived; by the end of 1970 the recession had, in fact, ended.

Reducing the cost

One can see that there is a cost to fighting inflation. This cost is in terms of the temporary increase in unemployment that results when monetary growth is slowed. The Prices and Incomes Commission has argued that this economic cost translates into a political cost (losing office) which many politicians view as so high that they are unwilling to fight inflation. Anything which can be found to reduce the costs of fighting inflation should be given serious consideration. The Commission advocated price and wage controls because, they thought, controls reduce the cost of fighting inflation. Wage and price controls alone do not fight inflation. But it is argued that when wage and price controls are introduced along with a policy of slower monetary growth, the inflation rate will be reduced and the resulting temporary increase in unemployment will be less than the unemployment that results when reduced monetary growth is the only policy used.[36]

Create the illusion

It is argued that the announcement of a policy of comprehensive and mandatory wage and price controls will convince the public that the government is serious in its fight against inflation. In turn, this will lead the public to believe that the government will, in fact, reduce the inflation rate and as a consequence the public will revise downward its expectations of inflation. When reduced monetary growth is also accompanied by reduced expectations of inflation there will be a reduction in the temporary increase in the rate of unemployment that occurs whenever monetary growth is reduced. In this way wage and price controls reduce the costs of fighting inflation. In the eyes of the Commission, wage and price controls must be introduced along with a policy of reduced monetary growth. "It is our view. . . that temporary price and income controls should only be used as part of a longer-run policy aimed at maintaining underlying demand conditions both during and after the control period consistent with the target rates of increase in average price and income levels."[37]

Expectations

The arguments of the Prices and Incomes Commission can not be dismissed off hand. They do not depend upon any faulty theoretical framework. The crux of their argument lies in the effect of the announcement of wage and price controls on the expectations of inflation. The crucial question to ask is: why does the announcement of wage and price controls affect expectations of inflation? Wage and price controls do not affect inflation, why should they therefore affect expectations of inflation? It is the reduced growth in the money supply that reduces the inflation rate. If the government desired a positive announcement effect the solution would be easy. The Prime Minister could go on coast-to-coast radio and television and announce that the government was going to follow a policy of reduced monetary growth. If the public believes the government, expectations of inflation will be reduced. This policy would have a tremendous advantage over wage and price controls. It would not entail all the costs of controls. (A discussion of these costs appears in Section IV.) Suppose it is argued that the public does not understand the underlying cause of inflation. Should they associate wage and price controls with reduced inflation? The answer is obviously no. In the previous section we saw that wage and price controls have never been successful in fighting inflation. If they never have worked is it reasonable to believe, that the Canadian public will assume controls will work now. There is no reason to assume this and no reason to believe controls will reduce expectations of inflation.†

Fooling whom?

In fact, there is some evidence to believe that controls may ultimately lead to higher rather than lower inflation rates. Controls take the government's attention away from the use of monetary policy to fight inflation. If the government is fooled by the illusionary success of wage and price controls they may not feel it necessary to follow a policy of reduced monetary growth. They may thus allow a higher monetary growth rate than they would have if there were no controls. Darby argues that this was the case with the U.S. experience with controls. During and after Phase II, money supply grew at excessive rates and this subsequently resulted in higher rates of inflation in the U.S. economy. If this phenomenon generally occurs when controls are enacted, then controls may result in higher rather than lower expectations of inflation.

The results of this section are fairly straightforward. Controls can not affect the inflation rate. It is highly unlikely that controls reduce inflationary expectations. As a result, controls will not reduce the costs of fighting inflation. Wage and price controls are a policy that yield no substantial benefits to the economy as a whole. The main problem with controls is not their ineffectiveness in dealing with the inflation problem; the main problem lies in the potentially high costs that controls impose on a free market economy.

IV. WHAT PRICE WAGE AND PRICE CONTROLS?

The main problem with controls is that they interfere in a detrimental way with the determination of individual prices[38] and wages. How much interference takes place and how much damage is done depends crucially on a number of factors: how comprehensive the control system is, how rigidly the controls are enforced and how monetary policy is behaving while controls are being imposed.

---

†Editor's note: The study by Professor Michael Parkin in this series concludes, on the basis of experience in the U.S. and the U.K., that ". . . inflation expectations . . . are not influenced by the presence or absence of controls".

First, let us consider the case where controls are imposed along with a policy of reducing the rate of growth of the money supply. Suppose controls allowed prices and wages to increase by 8 per cent per year and the money supply was growing at a rate consistent with 5 per cent inflation. The controls in this case would not matter for most prices. For most goods and services the ceiling increase in wages and prices would be greater than the increase that would be determined by the operation of free markets. As such, for most goods, the controls will not be binding and will not affect the determination of individual prices. However, there will be some goods whose equilibrium prices would increase by more than 8 per cent if free markets were allowed.

In a dynamic economy, demand for, and supplies of, goods and services are constantly changing and therefore relative prices are constantly changing. In an inflationary world this means that some prices will be increasing at rates faster than the economy-wide inflation rate and some prices will be increasing at rates slower than this rate. For those commodities needing price increases greater than 8 per cent, the controls will be binding causing distortion in the allocation of resources and distribution of output. This distortion will be investigated in detail shortly. For now all that needs to be said is that in this case the distortion is likely to be small since controls are only binding for a small number of commodities.

In the case where controls are imposed in conjunction with a policy of reduced monetary growth the costs of the controls are likely to be minor. The question to be asked in this case is what is the purpose of having the controls? It is the reduction in money growth that reduces inflation. Controls offer no benefits and involve minor costs. In this case controls have no *raison d'être*. The reduction in monetary growth is the only useful policy tool.

The Canadian case

Now let us consider the case where excessive monetary growth has caused inflation. Let us assume that in this environment the government imposes binding controls and does not change monetary policy. Before investigating this case it should be noted that it is highly likely that current

Canadian controls will fit into this scenario. In Prime Minister Trudeau's speech to the nation, on October 13, 1975, announcing wage and price controls he emphasized again and again the need for every group in the economy to reduce their money income demands. Nowhere did he state that the monetary policy of the government would change. In fact, he didn't even indicate any significant change in fiscal policy. From this speech it would appear that wage and price controls are the government's sole weapon in its fight against inflation and that the government does not intend to change monetary policy in the foreseeable future.†

For controls to affect individual prices they must be binding: i.e. the controlled ceiling price must be below the price that would be set in the free market. The Canadian control scheme allows wages to increase by 8 per cent per year in the first year of a contract to compensate for inflation. In successive years the allowable wage increases will diminish. With inflation currently running around 11 per cent, and likely to continue at that level for the foreseeable future, Canadian controls will be binding on wage contracts. As time goes on the controls will become more and more severe since allowable wage increases will diminish. Prices under the Canadian scheme will, for a number of companies, be allowed to go up only enough to enable firms to recover increased costs. In this way the dollar amount of profits per unit of output will be frozen. With inflation continuing in excess of 10 per cent per year this fixed dollar amount of profits per unit of output will be worth less and less in real terms. Hence, allowable price increases will be less than would have taken place in the free market. On the whole it would appear that the Canadian control system is binding and will become more and more severe as time goes on. Hence, the following analysis would seem to be relevant for the Canadian case.

---

†Editor's Note: On September 22, 1975 the Governor of the Bank of Canada, G.K. Bouey indicated that the Bank of Canada intended to pursue a contractionary course. As ever, it was difficult to penetrate the cloud of Bank of Canada-ese in which the message was contained, but the message was certainly there. The key question is whether the government in fact understands and agrees with Mr. Bouey's position.

The matzo ball — fringe benefit syndrome

Let us proceed with the case where binding controls are imposed on an economy following an inflationary monetary policy. The first thing to notice is that controls interfere with the rights of individuals to receive income. Controls attempt to limit wage income, profit income, dividend income and so on. The first response of individuals and firms will be to try to legally evade the controls, where possible. In a number of cases this will be possible. In any transaction there is a large number of dimensions. Price controls only fix price to the quantity of goods. The other dimensions are left free to respond to economic conditions. Quality is one of these dimensions; the imposition of price controls often leads to a deterioration in quality. The imposition of rent controls inevitably causes the landlord to reduce maintenance expense on rented accommodations. Restaurants can easily alter recipes or reduce the size of their portions. Manufacturers can reduce the quality of their product. George Meany claimed that when price controls were introduced in the U.S. a well known manufacturer of matzo-ball soup reduced the number of matzo balls from four to three.† In the U.S. control period service station attendants started charging for putting air in tires and for cleaning windshields.

There are a number of dimensions of wage contracts that can be altered in response to wage controls. Not all fringe benefits are included in wage controls; instead of wage increases firms can increase fringe benefits. The number of hours in the working week can be altered. The number of hours of overtime (at higher rates) can be increased relative to the number of standard hours. Promotions with higher pay are almost always allowed under controls. Firms can make Grade B mechanics Grade A mechanics. Universities can make associate professors full professors.

Round-trip rump roast

Also, under controls, there is always a list of products which are exempt from the controls or there are products on which

---

†Editor's Note: This allegation was subsequently refuted by Dr. Jackson Grayson, then Chairman of the Price Commission in the U.S., and a contributor to this Fraser Institute series; the point made in the allegation is, nevertheless, well-taken.

the controls are not binding. This being the case, firms can use tie-in sales to get around the controls. They will only sell the controlled item provided the uncontrolled item is purchased too. The total price charged for the package is the price that would have prevailed in the free market. Again firms can attempt to transform items from the controlled list to the uncontrolled list. In the U.S. control system exports of cattle and imports of beef were exempt. As a consequence, U.S. cattle ranchers sold their cattle to slaughterhouses in Canada at free market prices. The slaughtered cattle were then shipped from Canada to the U.S. at free market prices. This device enabled cattle ranchers to sell cattle at prices above the control prices.

As one can see there are a large number of legal ways of getting around the controls. With any new set of controls, I have no doubt that individuals will find new and ingenious loopholes. Canada's new system of controls, I am sure, will provide its own stories of evasion for future generations of economic professors to tell their students.

When controls are evaded, transaction prices for the same quality good will have risen but measured prices will not change. The official statistics will unwittingly underestimate the true inflation in the economy. The controls will merely suppress the symptoms of inflation. Evasion of controls prevents the distortion in allocation of resources and distribution of output that normally comes with controls. The problem is that this evasion is not without cost. It takes ingenuity to figure out ways around the controls. It takes resources to have cattle go on a round-trip journey from the U.S. to Canada. This resource cost is due solely to the imposition of wage and price controls. Without controls these resources would be free to provide additional goods and services.

Shortages and queues

There will be goods and services for which the evasion costs will outweigh the benefits from evasion. For these goods and services the controlled prices will prevail. The controlled price will be less than the price that would exist in the absence of controls. The low control price will encourage consumption and at the same time discourage production of the good.[39] At the low controlled price the quantity demanded will exceed the quantity of the good supplied. Under free markets the price would rise to balance supply and demand or clear the market. As the price rose demand for the good would decrease and supply would increase. The price would rise until the amount of the good people desired to purchase would just equal the amount of the good firms desired to sell. It is in this way that the market clears. Under price controls, however, price can not clear the market. Some other mechanism must be used to ration the existing supply of goods to those desiring to purchase them.

In the absence of other methods, products will be rationed on a first come, first served basis. Not all customers will get the quantity of the goods they want. Shortages will develop. People will line up to purchase goods. Time costs in making transactions will increase substantially. Transactions which formerly were taken for granted will now require substantial amounts of time. The increased transaction time will either reduce time spent in leisure activities or time spent producing goods and services.

A most stunning example of queues comes from the recent U.S. experience with controls on gasoline prices. At the controlled price of gasoline there was a shortage. As a consequence of this shortage people filled up with gasoline whenever they could. Many gasoline stations rationed supplies by limiting gasoline purchases to five gallons. As a result of all this, queues for gasoline became intolerable. People had to wait upwards of two hours to purchase five gallons of gasoline. If it takes two hours to purchase five gallons of gasoline at 50 cents per gallon and if people's time is worth $5.00 an hour then the total cost of gasoline (including time cost) was $2.50 per gallon. Under controls, the total cost of gasoline was probably at an all-time high for the U.S. economy. It shouldn't be surprising to learn that some individuals went into the business of waiting in line and filling up cars with gasoline. While the true cost of gasoline skyrocketed the measured price showed no change. This is just another case where the official price has no meaning whatever. Imagine if every product were marketed like gasoline. Individuals would spend all their time in making transactions and very little time in producing new goods and services. The phenomenon of queuing is wasteful of resources and as a consequence causes output to be less than it would be in the absence of controls.

Rationing

When queues become so long and so wasteful of resources, the government inevitably introduces formal rationing schemes. By some method the existing output is allocated to the consumer. Since the allocation is done by government officials, the allocation procedure is formulated under great political pressure. Under formal rationing, each of the 22 million Canadians will argue that they are 'special' cases and they deserve generous quotas. Everyone will act in a way that makes it very difficult to ration the existing quantity of output. Under the price system, the price will rise and provide an incentive for individuals to cut back on consumption of this good and provide an incentive for firms to increase production. Under the price system, all 22 million Canadians have an incentive to act in such a way that the market is cleared. Under formal rationing, groups with large amounts of political power will receive relatively large amounts of the rationed goods. Formal rationing schemes generally involve the issuing of ration coupons. These ration coupons are valuable commodities and in a short time a market in these coupons is established (whether it be legal or not). Prices will be established for ration coupons of various types. In this case the price of any good is equal to the money price of that good plus the price of the ration coupon needed to purchase the good. Again, in this case measured prices will underestimate true transaction prices.

It should be noted that when shortages develop, be there a formal rationing scheme or not, there will be consumers who do not get all the quantity of the good they want. Those unsatisfied consumers will search for substitute products. If any of the substitute products are not subject to controls then these products will experience higher than normal price increases. In this case excess demand pressure shifts to the non-controlled items.

Black markets

Inevitably shortages lead to the development of black markets. At the controlled price there will be a group of unsatisfied buyers; i.e., buyers who were unable to purchase their desired amount of the good. Some of these buyers will be willing to pay a price higher than the controlled one. Sellers will soon discover this and if this price is high enough to warrant engaging in illegal activities, black markets will be formed. Black markets existed in Canada during the control period of the Second World War. Black markets are common in the Communist countries of Eastern Europe. In Russia the penalty for economic crimes (i.e. black market transactions) is death. In spite of this penalty there is an active black market in Russian rubles in Austria. Black markets are almost impossible to eliminate. Of course, black market transactions do not get into the official statistics. Again, this is a case where measured prices underestimate actual prices.

In the above discussion we have seen that even with controls most people and firms will manage to buy and sell in a way that best suits them. Suppliers will manage to get a price for their products that is very close to the market price. Buyers will somehow get the products that they want. Economists summarize this by saying that even in the presence of controls the market will clear — supply and demand will balance.

The market always has to clear. But the crucial question is how this clearing takes place. Under the price system, price is the instrument which balances the supply and demand sides of the market; price rations the goods. Under controls the market may be cleared in a variety of ways. With legal evasion of controls, it is changes in dimensions of goods other than quantity (quality, for example) which clear the market. Of course when quality falls the effective price rises and accordingly, quality variation is really disguised price change.

When shortages develop, goods may be rationed by waiting or by formal rationing schemes. With black markets price rations the goods but the costs of dealing in black markets are different than the costs of dealing in free markets. Both in free and unfree markets, market forces always balance. The question to be answered is why should one system of market clearance be preferred over the other? To answer this question we first have to investigate the role that prices (and wages) perform in the free market economy.[40]

The role that prices play

In the free market system consumers spend their money income according to the relative importance they attach to the various goods.[41] In the free market system it is assumed that the individual knows his own tastes best. Individuals will be willing to offer high prices for goods that rank high in their preference scale and low prices for goods ranking low on their preference scale. Firms will compete with one another to produce goods whose price gives them the largest return over the value of the productive resources required to produce them. Firms which produce goods that are not in demand will be unable to sell them. In this way firms are compelled to produce goods which are in demand. "Producers therefore find it profitable to utilize productive power to make the things the public needs or wants, in the correct proportions."[42]

In this free market economy, suppose consumer tastes change and people place more value on a particular good than they used to. Effectively, the demand for the good increases. At the existing price, demand for the good will exceed its supply. This will cause prices to rise: the rising price will reduce demand somewhat but in addition it will make it more profitable to produce this good. This higher profitability will enable producers of this good to pay higher prices for labour, material, etc. and attract these resources away from their alternative uses. These additional resources will enable firms producing this good (whose demand has increased) to increase their production. In this way "the preferences of consumers will pull (reward) resources to the uses of highest value, indicated by the higher prices (as signals) in the favored market."[43] Price thus directs production and resources according to the wants and the needs of the public.

The price system also dictates that goods should be produced as efficiently as possible. Firms compete with one another in the production of goods and in the acquiring of resources. Those firms who can produce the greatest output with a given amount of resources can afford to pay the highest prices for these resources. They can thus force their competitors out of business or force them to use efficient methods also. "Thus every detail in the production process is constantly subjected to a ruthless process of selection in a struggle for existence, and an irresistible pressure is brought to bear toward the use of productive power both in the 'best direction' and in accord with methods of the highest possible efficiency."[44]

Double-barrelled signals

In the price system, goods are produced according to consumer wants and in the most efficient ways possible. To achieve this result prices (including the prices of resources such as labour) play a crucial role. They serve a dual function. In one role, prices transmit information. They serve as signals from consumers to producers directing firms to the production of those goods which consumers desire. They serve as signals from producers to owners of resources. Resources are directed to those goods in which they are needed the most. In their second role, prices provide an incentive for people and firms to act on the basis of the information inherent in the price signals. Firms that produce products not in demand, with a price low in relation to the costs of production, will lose money and eventually go out of business. Firms that produce products in demand will be rewarded with profits and will be allowed to stay in business. Owners of resources sending those resources to their most productive uses will be rewarded with high prices for these resources.

Short-circuiting the mechanism

In this way prices play a crucial role in the efficient allocation of resources and the distribution of output. How is this role affected by the imposition of wage and price controls? When goods are rationed by waiting or by formal rationing schemes the crucial role that prices play in the economy is suppressed. When demand exceeds supply the wants of consumers are dictating that more of this good should be produced. If price is not allowed to go up, more of this good will not be produced. With price controls, goods will not necessarily be produced according to the wants and needs of the public. When demand exceeds supply for a particular product this indicates that resources can be more productively used in the provision of that product rather than some other products. Since prices of resources are not allowed to be bid up, resources will not flow to the goods in which they are needed the most. In addition, since efficient firms can not bid resources away from the inefficient firms, there is no guarantee that resources will be used as productively as possible.

Breaking the thermometer

Milton Friedman in looking for an analogy for wage and price controls, makes the point that

"An analogy is often drawn between direct control of wages and prices as a reaction to inflation and the breaking of a thermometer as a reaction to, say, an over-heated room. This analogy has an element of validity. Prices are partly like thermometers in that they register heat but do not produce it; in both cases, preventing a measuring instrument from recording what is occurring does not prevent the occurrence. But the analogy is misleading. Breaking the thermometer need have no further effect on the phenomenon being recorded; it simply adds to our ignorance. Controlling prices, insofar as it is successful, has very important effects. Prices are not only measuring instruments, they also play a vital role in the economic process itself. A much closer analogy is a steam-heating furnace running full blast. Controlling the heat in one room by closing the radiators in that room simply makes other rooms still more overheated. Closing all the radiators lets the pressure build up in the boiler and increases the danger that it will explode."[45]

Wage and price controls waste and misallocate resources. Resources are wasted in waiting when queues are used to ration supplies. Resources are wasted on administering and enforcing the controls. Resources are wasted in attempting to get around the controls either by legal or illegal means. Resources are misallocated. All of this causes a reduction in output. How great a reduction in output will take place in response to any particular control system is difficult to predict. The extent of the reduction in output depends on how much lower the control price is than the true equilibrium price, how rigidly the controls are enforced, how easy it is to get around controls and whether any formal rationing scheme is implemented along with the controls. The case of Germany after World War I and after World War II provides an interesting example of the costs of controls.

The German case

After World War I, Germany had an episode of hyperinflation. There were periods in the hyperinflation when prices were doubling every day. Throughout this hyperinflation individual prices were determined by market forces. Wage and price controls were never imposed. In spite of the large number of problems that hyperinflation caused, the amazing thing is that real output never declined until the last six months of the hyperinflation. One can attribute this to the fact that throughout the period resources were allocated using the price system. After World War II, Germany again experienced substantial inflation. This inflation, although considerable by Canadian standards, was mild in comparison to the hyperinflation experienced after World War I. In this second period of inflation, Germany imposed very severe wage and price controls which were rigidly enforced. In this period of German history when inflation was suppressed, output fell in half.[46] For Germany, the price of controls was indeed very high.

V. SUMMARY AND CONCLUSIONS

The following are the conclusions reached in this paper:

1. Inflation is the result of excessive growth in the money supply. Inflation is at all times and in all places a monetary phenomenon.

2. Wage and price controls will not reduce the true inflation rate. Controls do not get at the central cause of inflation. Controls merely mask the symptoms of inflation.

3. Controls confuse the issue as to the true cause of inflation and make the application of the correct policy to fight inflation (reducing the money supply) less likely.

4. Controls will not aid in reducing the costs of fighting inflation.

5. Controls waste and misallocate resources. This inefficiency results in a loss of output. The severity of the loss in output depends on the severity with which controls are applied and enforced.

Wage and price controls are a policy which offer no long-term benefits to the economy as a whole.[47] The cost of the controls can vary anywhere from that of a minor nuisance to that of a major economic disaster. From an economic point of view a policy that yields no benefits and potentially high costs is a policy that should be rejected out of hand. This clearly has not happened in Canada. The enactment of wage and price controls by the current government is an economic mistake. The irony of the situation is that the current policy represents a complete turnaround for the government. In the election campaign of the summer of 1974 the government correctly weighed up the costs and benefits of controls and firmly opposed compulsory wage and price controls. The inflation rate in the fall of 1975 was the same as in the summer of 1974. The arguments that were valid in 1974 are equally valid today: ". . . wage and price controls aren't new. They aren't innovative. They aren't magic. They have been tried and tried and always found wanting. Wage and price controls do not work. The distortions they create, the shortages they develop and the pent-up pressure for wages unleash more serious problems than those the controls set out to solve."[48]

Notes

[1] For a discussion of this period in history see H. Michell, "The Edict of Diocletian: A Study of Price Fixing in the Roman Empire," *Canadian Journal of Economics and Political Science*, February 1947, p. 1-13.

[2] For a description of these controls see K.W. Taylor, "Canadian War-time Price Controls, 1941-6," *Canadian Journal of Economics and Political Science*, February 1947, p. 81-99.

[3] In England and on the continent these controls go under the name 'incomes policy.'

[4] See M. Parkin, "Wage-Price Controls: The Lessons from Britain," in this series for a discussion of wage and price controls in England. For a discussion of controls in Europe see L. Ulman and R. J. Flannagan, *Wage Restraint: A Study of Incomes Policy in Western Europe*, Berkeley and Los Angeles, 1971.

[5] For a discussion of the various phases of U.S. controls see M. Darby, "The U.S. Economic Stabilization Program of 1971-1974," in this Fraser Institute series.

[6] Fifty to one hundred years ago 'inflation' referred to inflation of currency and not to the resulting inflation in prices.

[7] Economists generally do not worry about inflation rates below 2 per cent. Since quality changes tend to be underestimated in calculating the C.P.I., an increase in the measured C.P.I. of less than 2 per cent could well indicate no change or a decrease in the true C.P.I.

[8] When the inflation rate reaches a level say around 50 per cent per month economists call this 'hyperinflation.' Germany after the First World War is an example of an economy in hyperinflation.

[9] The definition of the money supply that will be used throughout this paper will be currency in circulation plus all Canadian dollar deposits in chartered banks excluding Federal government deposits.

[10] *Final Report*, Prices and Incomes Commission. Information Canada, 1972, p. 60-63.

[11] P. Cagan, "Inflation and Market Structure, 1967-73," *Explorations in Economic Research*, Spring 1975.

[12] It should be noted that there are many variants of cost or price-push inflation. One can almost find a variant of cost-push theories corresponding to every type of cost. In addition various types of price-pushes have been identified in the literature (e.g., administered price inflation, mark-up inflation and so on).

[13] Text of Prime Minister Pierre Trudeau's radio and television address to the nation as reported in the *Toronto Globe and Mail*, October 14, 1975.

[14] Keynes adopted this proposition and it was advocated by the Keynesian economists of the period. For support of this proposition see J.M. Keynes, *The General Theory of Employment, Interest and Money*, Macmillan , Co., London, 1961, p. 295-6.

[15]A.W. Phillips, "The Relation between Unemployment and the Rate of Change in Money Wage Rates in the United Kingdom, 1861-1957," *Economica*, November 1958.

[16]Workers may temporarily supply more labour if they have not yet realized that prices have doubled. In the short-run when inflation increases and this increase is not recognized by all workers, the unemployment rate may temporarily decline.

[17]It should be pointed out that middlemen perform valuable services in reducing the costs of acquiring information about products and in reducing other buying costs, like transportation, of consumers. Even pure speculators provide a valuable service by transferring a good from a time of plenty where society doesn't value it highly to a time of scarcity where the value of the good has increased.

[18]The monetary theory of inflation generally goes under the name of the 'quantity theory' of inflation.

[19]For a discussion of these lags in Canada, see J.L. Carr, "The Money Supply and the Rate of Inflation," in *Essays in Monetary Aspects of Inflation*, Nold, Carr and Winder, Information Canada, 1973.

[20]Also during these periods the average number of weeks income in money balances that people desired to hold changed one quarter of one per cent per year.

[21]Since there are lags in the effects of monetary policy the period used to look at the inflation rate will start and end one year later than the period used in defining monetary policy.

[22]Advocates of the monetary theory of inflation, in general, do not believe in the concept of a Phillips Curve in terms of permanently trading-off more unemployment for less inflation. However most would agree that when a reduction in the money supply occurs, in the short-run, inflation will be reduced and unemployment increased. Hence they believe in a short-run Phillips Curve but not in a long-run Phillips Curve.

[23]Anna Schwartz, "Secular Price Change in Historical Perspective," *Journal of Money, Credit and Banking*, February 1973.

[24]Milton Friedman, "What Price Guideposts," in *Guidelines: Informal Controls and the Market Place*, ed. by G.P. Shultz and R.Z. Aliber, University of Chicago Press, 1966, p. 18.

[25]In Canada the money supply is controlled by the Bank of Canada. The Bank of Canada can not for very long follow a monetary policy which is contrary to the wishes of the government of the day. It is for this reason we speak of the Federal government controlling monetary policy.

[26]By 'tight money' I mean a policy of relatively small rates of increase in the money supply.

[27]In Canada only the Federal government has the power to issue money. As a consequence this avenue of finance is not open to provincial and municipal governments.

[28]A case may be made why government deficits financed by debt issue may lead to a once and for all increase in the price level. Government debt issue may increase interest rates. This leads to a decrease in the demand for money. People attempting to spend excess money balance will cause the price level to rise. It should be noted that this will only cause a once and for all rise in the price level and not continual inflation.

[29]It should be noted that the argument that controls are ineffective in combatting inflation does not depend on the validity of the monetary theory of inflation. If we believed in demand-pull inflation, that increases in nominal aggregate demand, no matter what the source, are responsible for inflation then the argument could still be made that controls are ineffective in reducing inflation.

[30]A case can be made that wage and price controls may reduce the reported inflation rate in the short-run. This issue will be discussed in Section IV of this paper.

[31]M. Darby, *op. cit.*

[32]M. Parkin, *op. cit.*

[33]R.G. Lipsey and M. Parkin, "Incomes Policy: A Re-appraisal," in *Incomes Policy and Inflation*, ed. by M. Parkin and M.T. Sumner, Manchester University Press, 1972, p. 85.

[34]*Final Report*, Prices and Incomes Commission. Information Canada, 1972. Appendix B, p. 7.

[35]It should be noted that this is only one possible reason why unemployment results when the rate of growth of the money supply is reduced. For other possible reasons why this may occur see E. Phelps, "The New Microeconomics in Employment and Inflation Theory," in E. Phelps, *Microeconomic Foundations of Employment and Inflation Theory*, W.W. Norton & Co., New York, 1970.

[36]In technical terms it is argued that wage and price controls make the short-run Phillips Curve steeper.

[37]*Final Report*. Prices and Incomes Commission. Information Canada, 1972. Appendix B., p. 48.

[38]The term individual prices and relative prices is used interchangeably in this study.

[39]This statement is not entirely correct for the case where controls are imposed on a monopolized product. In this case it is possible that initially when controls are imposed output will increase not decrease. As time progresses and the controlled prices changes more and more from the market price, it becomes more and more likely that output of the monopolized good will decrease.

[40]For a discussion of this issue see F. Knight, *The Economic Organization*, Harper & Row, 1965.

[41]Consumers rank relative importance at the prices for which the various goods are offered.

[42]F. Knight, *op. cit.*, p. 34.

[43]Roger Weiss, *The Economic System*, Random House, New York, 1968, p. 28.

[44]Frank Knight, *op. cit.*, p. 34.

[45]Milton Friedman, *op. cit.*, p. 19-20.

[46]It should be admitted that not all of this fall in output can be attributed to price controls. Germany suffered greater war damage in the Second World War than in the first.

[47]One may ask how a policy with no benefits to the economy as a whole can be enacted by government. The answer must lie in the fact that some groups in the economy expect benefits from controls. If these groups have enough political power they can get controls enacted.

[48]Boyd Upper, Ontario Liberal party policy chairman, Speech to Ontario Liberal Candidates' College, May 18, 1974, York University.

PART II

have controls ever worked?

The Historical Record

A Survey of Wage and Price Controls Over Fifty Centuries

ROBERT SCHUETTINGER

Lecturer in Economics
Yale University

THE AUTHOR

Robert L. Schuettinger was born in New York in 1936 and studied at Columbia, Oxford, Chicago (M.A.) and St. Andrews (B.Phil.) Universities. An avid student of liberal thought, Professor Schuettinger studied under Friedrich Hayek at Chicago and Sir Isaiah Berlin at Oxford.

His historical scholarly works include *The Conservative Tradition in European Thought*, (Putnam's, New York, 1970) and a biography of Lord Acton to be published by Open Court, 1976.

Professor Schuettinger has taught at the Catholic University of America, the New School for Social Research and St. Andrews University. Presently, Professor Schuettinger teaches at Yale University and is a Senior Research Associate to the Republican Study Committee in the U.S. House of Representatives.

The Historical Record

A Survey of
Wage and Price Controls
Over Fifty Centuries

ROBERT SCHUETTINGER

Lecturer in Economics
Yale University

I. THE ANCIENT WORLD

From earliest times, from the first days of organized government, rulers and their officials have attempted, with varying degrees of success, to 'control' their economies. The idea that there is a 'just' or 'fair' price for a certain good or a certain kind of labor which can and ought to be enforced by government is apparently as old as civilization.

For the past forty-six centuries at least, governments all over the world have periodically tried to fix wages and prices. When their efforts failed, as they usually did, governments then put the blame on the wickedness of their subjects.

The passion for economic planning, as Professor John Jewkes of Oxford University has cogently pointed out,[1] is perennial. Centralized planning regularly appears in every generation and is just as readily discarded after several years of experimentation. Grandiose plans for regulating investment, wages, prices and production are usually unveiled with great fanfare and high hopes. As reality gradually seeps in, the plans are first modified, then drastically altered and

59

finally quietly allowed to vanish unmourned. Human nature being what it is, every decade or so the same old plans are dusted off (perhaps given a different name) and the process, like spring following winter, begins anew.

As early as the fifth dynasty in Egypt, generally dated at about 2800 B.C., the Monarch Henku had inscribed on his tomb "I was lord and overseer of southern grain in this nome."

For centuries the Egyptian government strove to maintain control of the grain crop, knowing that control of the people's food would necessarily mean control of their lives. Using the pretext of preventing famine, the government gradually regulated more and more granaries; regulation led to direction and finally to outright ownership; land became the property of the monarch and was rented from him by the agricultural class.[2]

In Babylon, about 4,000 years ago, the Code of Hammurabi imposed a rigid system of controls over wages and prices. The entire economy of Babylon was subject to minute regulation in all its aspects.[3]

On the other side of the world, the rulers of ancient China shared the same paternalistic philosophy to be found among the Egyptians and Babylonians and later, among the Greeks and Romans.

Confucius says

According to the Chinese scholar, Dr. Huan-Chang Chen, the economic doctrines of Confucius taught that "there are two sets of interest, those of producers and those of consumers. But nothing more markedly affects the interests of both sides at once than prices. Therefore, price is the great problem for society as a whole. According to the Confucian theory, the government should level prices by the adjustment of demand and supply, in order to guarantee the cost of the producer and satisfy the wants of the consumer . . . *It is the task of the superior man to adjust demand and supply so as to keep prices on a level."*[4] (emphasis added)

The officials of the ancient Chinese Empire expected to do what members of their class have perennially attempted before and since, in other times and other places. They hoped to replace the natural laws of supply and demand with their own superior judgement of what the 'proper' supply and the 'proper' demand ought to be.

Dr. Chen relates that "according to the official system of Chou (about 1122 B.C.), the superintendent of grain looked around the fields and determined the amount of grain to be collected or issued, in accordance with the condition of the crop; fulfilling the deficit of their demand and adjusting their supply."

As might be expected, however, this high-minded system did not always work as perfectly as intended since even mandarins are human and thus subject to error and occasional corruption. Dr. Chen concludes dryly that "the chief difficulty in administering (production, price and wage controls) is that it is not easy for officials to undertake commercial functions along with political duties."[5]

Greek experience

During the Golden Age of Athens, in the time of Socrates and Plato, the bureaucrats of the Acropolis were even less successful than their Oriental counterparts in interfering with the laws of supply and demand.

As a populous city-state with a small hinterland, Athens was constantly short of grain, at least half of which had to be imported from overseas. There was, needless to say, a natural tendency for the price of grain to rise when it was in short supply and to fall when there was an abundance. An army of grain inspectors, who were called Sitephylaces, was appointed for the purpose of setting the price of grain at a level the Athenian government thought to be just.

The result was as might be expected. Despite the penalty of death, which the harassed government did not hesitate to inflict, the laws controlling the grain trade were almost impossible to enforce. We have an 'oration' from at least one of the frustrated Athenian politicians who implored a jury to put the offending merchants to death. "But it is necessary, gentlemen of the jury", he urged, "to chastise them not only for the sake of the past, but also as an example for the future; for as things now are they will hardly be endurable. And consider that in consequence of this vocation very many already have stood trial for their life; and so great are the emoluments which they derive from it that they prefer to risk their life every day rather than cease to draw from you unjust profits . . . If then you shall condemn them, you shall act justly and you will buy grain cheaper; otherwise dearer."[6]

Lysias was not the first and he was hardly the last politician to court popularity by promising the people lower prices in times of scarcity if only they would hang a few merchants. The Athenian government, in fact, went so far as to execute their own inspectors who did not enforce the price ceiling with sufficient zeal. Despite the high death rates for merchants and bureaucrats alike, the price of grain still rose when demand exceeded supply and ultimately the system collapsed.[7]

Times Roman

The most famous and the most extensive attempt to control prices and wages occurred in the reign of the Emperor Diocletian who, to the considerable regret of his subjects, was not the most attentive student of Greek economic history. Since both the causes of the inflation that Diocletian attempted to control and the effects of his efforts are well documented it is an episode worth considering in some detail.[8]

The historical backdrop against which Diocletian's reign must be viewed was probably "the most unhappy and intolerable century in which mankind has suffered for the ambitions of headstrong men."[9] It was an epoch marked by utter anarchy as first one army and then another pillaged its way through the provinces of the Empire. The struggle for power and the maintenance of larger armies to keep it led to the total bankruptcy of the Empire. In vain attempts to satisfy the enormous requirements of the army, successive emperors piled tax upon tax, confiscated the wealth of opponents and minted enormous quantities of an increasingly worthless currency. In short, "The Empire was clearly breaking up in misery and confusion, bankruptcy and anarchy."[10]

The principal instrument of villainy was without question the debasement of the currency. During the fifty year interval ending with the rule of Claudius Victorinus in 268

A.D. the silver content of the Roman coin fell to one five-thousandth of its original level. With the monetary system in total disarray, the trade which had been a hallmark of the Empire was reduced to barter and economic activity was stymied. "The middle class was almost obliterated and the proletariat was quickly sinking to the level of serfdom. Intellectually the world had fallen into an apathy from which nothing could rouse it."[11] To this intellectual and moral morass came the Emperor Diocletian and he set about the task of reorganization with great vigor. Unfortunately, his zeal exceeded his understanding of the economic forces at work in the Empire.

In an attempt to overcome the paralysis associated with centralized bureaucracy, he decentralized the administration of the Empire and created three new centres of power under three 'associate emperors.' Since money was completely worthless, he devised a system of taxes based on payments in kind. This system had the effect, via the *ascripti glebae*, of totally destroying the freedom of the lower classes — they became serfs and were bound to the soil to ensure that the taxes would be forthcoming.

The 'reforms' that are of most interest, however, are those relating to the currency and prices and wages. The currency reform came first and was followed, after it had become clear that the currency reform was a failure, by the Edict on prices and wages. Diocletian had attempted to instil public confidence in the currency by putting a stop to the production of debased gold and silver coins. He devalued the denarius — the bronze currency of day-to-day commerce — so that it was worth half its former value in gold. Unfortunately, he did not have sufficient stocks of gold and silver to back the denarius, and it became widely known that the denarius was not worth what Diocletian said it was worth. The people were not fooled by the currency 'reform', black markets in gold and silver flourished and the 'reformed' monetary system was on the verge of collapse. Diocletian found himself on the horns of what is, in retrospect, a very familiar dilemma.

The principal reason for the official overvaluation of the currency was to provide the wherewithal to support the large army and massive bureaucracy — the equivalent of

modern government. His choices were to continue to mint
the increasingly worthless denarius or to cut 'government
expenditures' and thereby reduce the requirement for minting them. In modern terminology, he could either continue
to 'inflate' or he could begin the process of 'deflating' the
economy.

Diocletian judged that deflation, reducing the costs of
civil and military government, was impossible. On the other
hand:

> "To inflate would be equally disastrous in the long run.
> It was inflation that had brought the Empire to the
> verge of complete collapse. The reform of the currency
> had been aimed at checking the evil, and it was becom-
> ing painfully evident that it could not succeed in its
> task."[12]

Diocletian's Edict

It was in this seemingly desperate circumstance that Diocletian determined to continue to inflate, but to do so in a way
that would, he thought, prevent the inflation from occurring. He sought to do this by simultaneously fixing the prices
of goods and services and suspending the freedom of people
to decide what the official currency was worth. The famous
Edict of 301 A.D. was designed to accomplish this end.[13] Its
framers were very much aware of the fact that unless they
could enforce a universal value for the denarius in terms of
goods and services — a value that was wholly out of keeping
with its actual value — the system that they had devised
would collapse. Thus, the Edict was all pervasive in its
coverage and the penalties prescribed, severe.

From the available, known to be incomplete, portions
of the Edict we know that the 'values' in terms of the
denarius were fixed for 900 goods, 130 different grades of
labor and many freight rates. Thus, the prices of practically
all the goods the people of the Empire might wish to buy
were controlled. The penalty of death was prescribed (and
often enforced) for anyone who sold his goods for a higher
price. Wages were also fixed in every trade and profession
and anyone who charged a higher price for his services was
executed.

As was discussed above, the Edict was issued in an attempt to forestall the inevitable and, even then, well-known consequences of minting too much money. There can be no doubt that Diocletian knew full-well that the worthless denarius was at the root of the Empire's problems. This fact is reflected in the currency 'reform' that he undertook at the same time. There is also no doubt that he consciously set out to afix the blame for the inflation on others who were, willy-nilly, being carried along in the inflationary tide. He knew, and every government since him has known, that if his attempt to 'fool all the people' was to be successful the government must not be seen to be the cause of the inflation. Accordingly, he attempted to fix the blame on merchants of "immense fortunes who were greedy and full of a lust of plunder."

> "For who is so insensitive and so devoid of human feeling that he cannot know, or rather has not perceived, that in the commerce carried on in the markets . . . immoderate prices are so widespread that the uncurbed passion for gain is lessened neither by abundant supplies nor by fruitful years, so that without a doubt men who are busied in these affairs constantly plan actually to control the very winds and weather."[14]

The similarity between the gist of these remarks and that which 1600 years later is the rallying cry of modern governments bent on enforcing wage and price controls is devastating to behold.

Neither the Edict, nor the monetary 'reform' were successful. The price control Edict produced disastrous shortages of essential foodstuffs and was annulled.

> "There was also much blood shed upon very slight and trifling accounts, and the people brought provisions no more to markets, since they could not get a reasonable price for them and this increased the dearth so much, that at last after many had died by it, the law itself was laid aside."[15]

Less than four years after the currency reform associated with the Edict the price of gold in terms of the denarius had risen 250 per cent. Diocletian had failed to fool the people and had failed to suppress the ability of people to buy and sell as they saw fit. The failure of the Edict and the currency 'reform' led to a return to more conventional fiscal irresponsibility and by 305 A.D. the process of currency debasement had begun again.

By the turn of the century this process had produced a two thousand per cent increase in the price of gold in terms of denarii:

> "These are impossible figures and simply mean that any attempt at preserving a market, let alone a mint ratio, between the bronze denarius and the pound of gold was lost. The astronomical figures of the French 'assignats', the German mark after the First World War, and of the Hungarian pengo after the Second, were not unprecedented phenomena."[16] ". . . Copper coins could very easily be manufactured; numismatists testify that the coins of the fourth century often bear signs of hasty and careless minting; they were thrust out into circulation in many cases without having been properly trimmed or made tolerably respectable. This hasty manipulation of the mints was just as effective as our modern printing presses, with their floods of worthless, or nearly worthless, paper money."[17]

Although Diocletian's attempt to control the economy ended in complete failure and he was forced to abdicate, not sixty years later his successor, the Emperor Julian, was back at the same old stand. Edward Gibbon ironically notes that ". . . the Emperor ventured on a very dangerous and doubtful step of fixing, by legal authority, the value of corn (grain). He enacted that, in a time of scarcity, it should be sold at a price which had seldom been known in the most plentiful years; and that his own example might strengthen his laws (he sent into the market a large quantity of his own grain at the fixed price). The consequences might have been foreseen and were soon felt. The imperial wheat was purchased by the rich merchants; the proprietors of land, or of corn, withheld from that city the accustomed supply, and the small quantities that appeared in the market were secretly sold at an advanced and illegal price."[18]

The experience of Julian, like that of Diocletian before him, demonstrated again that attempts to control the laws of supply and demand produce the exact opposite of the desired effects.

II. FROM MEDIEVAL TO EARLY MODERN TIMES

During the Middle Ages, not only the national governments but also guilds and municipalities engaged in price-fixing as a normal activity. In the thirteenth century, officials in England "felt themselves bound to regulate every sort of economic transaction in which individual self-interest seemed to lead to injustice."[19]

In the year 1199 the government in London attempted to control the wholesale and retail price of wine. The law was difficult to enforce and eventually failed. In 1330 the passion for price-fixing stirred again and a new law was adopted requiring merchants to sell at a 'reasonable' price — this figure to be based upon importation costs plus other expenses. In a few years, due to changing economic conditions, the price of wine rose far above the 1330 price and the government finally had to accept defeat once again.[20]

The many efforts to regulate the prices of wheat and bread in England came to a similar conclusion. The first attempt was apparently made in 1202; the leading law in this case was 51 Henry III which fixed precise prices for varying weights of bread. The economic historian Simon Litman notes that "the law was enforced locally on sundry occasions, but fell gradually into disuse."[21]

"During the fourteenth and fifteenth centuries," the historian W.J. Ashley tells us, "parliament and the executive left the matter (of regulation of prices, place of sale, etc.) almost entirely in the hands of the local authorities . . . The municipal authorities frequently went beyond victuals, and regulated the prices of other articles of prime importance to the poorer classes, such as wood and coal, tallow and candles."[22]

During the reign of the Tudor dynasty (after 1485), Parliament "was not content with passing acts against practices which enhanced prices. It endeavoured to fix directly a fair price not only for victuals but also for other commodities."[23] Most of these regulations received little public support and gradually faded away.

Antwerp

In the sixteenth century misplaced economic controls were decisive in determining the fate of the most important city in what is now Belgium. From 1584 to 1585 Antwerp was besieged by Spanish forces led by the Duke of Parma who was intent on maintaining the rule of the Hapsburg Empire in the Lowlands. Naturally, during a siege, food quickly becomes a scarce commodity and prices accordingly rise. The City Fathers of Antwerp reacted as many others in their position have done before and since: they passed a law fixing a maximum price for each item of food. Severe penalties were prescribed for anyone who attempted to charge the market price. According to the historian John Fiske, the consequences of this policy were twofold:

> "It was a long time before the Duke of Parma, who was besieging the city, succeeded in so blockading the Scheldt as to prevent ships laden with eatables from coming in below. Corn and preserved meats might have been hurried into the beleaguered city by thousands of tons. But no merchant would run the risk of having his ships sunk by the Duke's batteries merely for the sake of finding a market no better than many others which could be reached at no risk at all . . . If provisions had brought a high price in Antwerp they would have been carried thither. As it was, the city by its own stupidity, blockaded itself far more effectually than the Duke of Parma could have done."

> "In the second place," Fiske concludes, "the enforced lowness of prices prevented any general retrenchment on the part of the citizens. Nobody felt it necessary to economize. So the city lived in high spirits until all at once provisions gave out . . ."[24]

In 1585 the city of Antwerp surrendered and was occupied by the forces of Spain.

Bengal

An even worse disaster, made more costly still by government bungling, occurred in the Indian province of Bengal in the eighteenth century. The rice crop in 1770 failed completely and fully a third of the population died. A number of scholars attribute this disaster primarily to the rigid policy of the government which was determined to keep the price of grains down rather than allowing it to rise to its natural level. A price rise, of course, would have been a natural rationing system permitting the available food to be stretched out until the next harvest. Without this rationing system, the reserve supplies were quickly consumed and millions died of hunger as a direct result.

For once in human history, however, government did learn by experience. Ninety-six years later the province of Bengal was again on the verge of famine. This time the procedure was completely different, as William Hunter relates:

"Far from trying to check speculation, as in 1770, the Government did all in its power to stimulate it . . . A government which, in a season of high prices, does anything to check speculation acts about as sagely as the skipper of a wrecked vessel who should refuse to put his crew upon half rations . . . In the earlier famine one could hardly engage in the grain trade without becoming amenable to the law. In 1866 respectable men in vast numbers went into the trade; for the Government, by publishing weekly returns of the rates in every district, rendered the traffic both easy and safe. Everyone knew where to buy grain cheapest and where to sell it dearest and food was accordingly bought from the districts which could best spare it and carried to those which most urgently needed it."[25]

The experience of Bengal, which had two failed harvests of major proportions within a century, provided a laboratory for testing the two policies. In the earlier case, price-fixing was enforced and a third of the people perished; in the latter case, the free market was allowed to function and the shortage was kept under control.

III. THE EARLY CANADIANS

The history of attempts to control wages and prices in the early days of Canadian settlement has not yet been well researched. Accordingly, the episodes reported here may represent only a sample out of a broad but unrecovered experience with controls. Most of the persons in authority in the early days of Canadian settlement were agents of some European government and it would be reasonable to suppose that these functionaries carried with them their homeland's propensities for economic controls.

Quebec

It is certain from some of the records that have been preserved that the internal trade of Quebec was minutely regulated. Of particular concern in the late 17th century were the comings and goings of itinerant merchants. In general they were forbidden to enter into retail transactions of any sort and were subject to no less than ten general prohibitions.[26] These regulations had the effect of a retail price maintenance law since they expressly forbad the competition of 'outsider' merchants. These itinerant merchants were excluded specifically because they would have reduced the price of goods and taken business from resident merchants. There is some indication in the subsequent record that the regulation was not an unqualified success. In 1727 the local (Quebec) merchants found it necessary to write to the king requesting that he suspend the operation of the itinerant merchants.[27] There is no evidence that this attempted interference was successful either. In fact, a memoir from the king dated April 19, 1729 contains a paragraph indicating the king's general support for the activities of the itinerant merchants.[28]

In 1689, the Superior Council of Quebec, following the long-established European practice, gave explicit permission to municipalities to regulate the price of bread. Although the exact effect of this regulation is not known, it can be supposed that all was not well and that a change in the baker's costs would have meant a shortage of bread. Perhaps it was a situation of this sort that led to price controls on wheat in the fall of 1700 — certainly, it was clearly indicated in the regulation of that year that the bakers would have, as a result of the order, to work for the city and were constrained from working in any other way.[29]

Louisbourg

During 1750 rules were made as to the price that must be charged for fresh cod fish. It was, by this order, explicitly forbidden for fishermen to refuse to sell their fish at the posted price provided only that the buyer was solvent. To appreciate the serious nature of this law, it is necessary to remember that the bulk of New France's wealth was derived from the cod fishery. Of course, from time to time this regulation lead to desperate circumstances for the fishermen and there is some reason to believe that it was responsible for the decline in the fishery in that area of New France.[30]

Canada's first economist?

The most interesting commentary on inflation that this early period in Canadian history yields is by a person or persons unknown writing in Quebec 19th April 1759. The passage, which is worth reprinting in its entirety, was written as a commentary appended to an exposition of the price of commodities in Canada. Having shown the rate of increase in the cost of most important commodities the writer went on to say:

> "The excessive expense which this picture presents is such that one has perhaps never seen before an example of it. And it comes less from real scarcity than from the enormous expenditures of the government which have multiplied paper money without any consideration for the stock of commodities nor for the number of consumers . . . The price of commodities has been rising step by step because of a similar step by step increase in the expenditures of the government. These expenditures, which one can estimate by the sum of bills of exchange drawn on the royal treasury, have mounted as follows:
> - in 1754 to 7 or 800 thousand livres
> - in 1755 to 4,000 thousand livres
> - in 1756 to 7 or 8,000 thousand livres
> - in 1757 to 13 or 14,000 thousand livres
> - in 1758 to 20 or 25,000 thousand livres.

Perhaps in this year of 1759 they will go up to 50 millions and more from whence it is easy to forsee what will be the price of commodities before January 1760. One estimates that in France there are 18 million people and 1,400 millions of circulating money which makes a sum of 75 livres per capita. In Canada one can only estimate about 80 thousand people and the circulation in the month of August was more than 30 millions which makes almost 400 livres per capita. Thus, the stock of commodities in Canada being in proportion with those of France, their price ought to be 6 times over and above that of France, since the representative signs (money) exceed by 6 times the things to be represented (goods). Now these notes being held in profusion by those who have a share in the business (government) they do not perceive the expensiveness of it all."[31]

There are several amazing things about this paragraph. The first is that the writer showed such insight into the economic problems of the country at that juncture. The second is the remarkable extent to which current circumstances are a repetition of the follies of that earlier time. It appears that we learn very little from experience.

IV. THE EARLY AMERICANS

The early New England colonists were convinced that government ought to extend its powers into the regulation of all aspects of society, from the religious to the political to the economic. "This was a defect of the age," the economic historian William Weeden tells us (though hardly a defect unique to seventeenth century Massachusetts) "but the Puritan legislator fondly believed that, once freed from the malignant influence of the ungodly, that once based upon the Bible, he could legislate prosperity and well-being for everyone, rich or poor."[32]

In 1630 the General Court made a fruitless attempt to fix wage rates. Carpenters, joiners, bricklayers, lawyers and thatchers were to receive no more than two shillings a day. A fine of ten shillings was to be levied against anyone who paid or received more.[33] In addition, "no commodity should be sold at above four pence in the shilling (33 per cent) more than it cost for ready money in England; oil, wine, etc., and cheese, in regard to the hazard of bringing, etc., (excepted)."[34]

Weeden comments dryly that "these regulations lasted about six months and were repealed."[35]

There was an attempt at about the same time to regulate trade with the Indians . . . with the same result. The price of beaverskins (an important article of trade at the time) was set at no more than 6 shillings a skin with a "fair" profit of 30 per cent plus cost of transportation. A shortage of corn, however, drove the price of that commodity up to 10 shillings "the strike", and sales of this dwindling supply to the Indians were prohibited. "Under this pressure, beaver advanced to 10 shillings and 20 shillings per pound; 'no corn, no beaver,' said the native. The Court was obliged to remove the fixed rate, and the price ruled at 20 shillings."[36]

The offshoot of the Massachusetts Bay Colony in Connecticut experienced the same artificial efforts to control prices and to divert trade from its natural courses. One nineteenth century historian has briefly summed up these attempts. "The New Haven colony," he wrote, "was made notorious by its minute inquisition into the details of buying and selling, of eating and dressing and of domestic difficulties. Then the people were mostly of one mind about the wisdom of such meddling, the community was small and homogeneous in population and religious sentiments. If such legislative interference could have been beneficent, here was a favourable opportunity. It failed utterly. The people were wise enough to see that it was a failure."[37]

The effects of controls on prices and wages were by no means confined to the English-speaking colonies in North America. In the territory that is now the State of Illinois, French settlers were faced with similar harassments from a far away government. In a history of that part of French North America, Clarence Alvord notes: "The imposition of minute regulations issued from Versailles had been a burden upon the beaver trade. Fixed prices for beavers of every quality that had to be bought, whatever the quantity, by the farmers at the Canadian ports, had made impossible a free development and had reduced the farmers one after another to the verge of bankruptcy . . . an order was issued on May 26, 1696, recalling all traders and prohibiting them from going thereafter into the wilderness . . . (though) complete enforcement of the decree was impossible."[38]

The sporadic attempts during the seventeenth and early eighteenth centuries to control the economic life of the American colonies increased in frequency with the approach of the War of Independence.

Not worth a Continental

One of the first actions of the Continental Congress in 1775 was to authorize the printing of paper money . . . the famous 'Continentals'. Pelatiah Webster, who was America's first economist, argued very cogently in a pamphlet published in 1776 that the new Continental currency would rapidly decline in value unless the issuance of paper notes was curbed. His advice went unheeded and, with more and more paper in circulation, consumers naturally began to bid up prices for a stock of goods that did not increase as fast as the money supply. By November, 1777, commodity prices had risen 480 per cent above the pre-war average.[39]

The Congress, however, at least when addressing the public, professed not to believe that their paper money was close to valueless but that prices had risen mainly because of unpatriotic speculators who were enemies of the government. "The real causes of advancing prices," one historian notes, "were as completely overlooked by that body as they were by Lysias when prosecuting the corn-factors of Greece. As the Greek orator wholly attributed the dearness of corn to a combination among the factors, so did Congress ascribe the enormous advance in the price of things to the action of those having commodities for sale."[40]

On November 19, 1776, the General Assembly of Connecticut felt impelled to pass a series of regulations providing for maximum prices for many of the necessaries of life. It also declared that "all other necessary articles not enumerated be in reasonable accustomed proportion to the above mentioned articles."[41] Another similar act was passed in May, 1777. By August 13, 1777, however, the unforeseen results of these acts became clear to the legislators and on that date both acts were repealed.[42]

In February 1778, however, the pro-regulation forces were again in the ascendancy and Connecticut adopted a new tariff of wages and prices. Retail prices were not to exceed wholesale prices by more than 25 per cent plus the cost of transportation.[43] In a few months it became evident once again that these controls would work no better than the former attempts and in June 1778, the Governor of Connecticut wrote to the President of the Continental Congress that these laws too, "had been ineffectual."[44]

The Connecticut experience, of course, was by no means unique. Massachusetts, among other states, went through almost exactly the same on-again, off-again syndrome with its own version of wage and price controls. In January 1777, a law was passed imposing "maximum prices for almost all the ordinary necessaries of life: food, fuel and wearing apparel, as well as for day labor . . . so far as its immediate aim was concerned," an historian concludes, "the measure was a failure."[45] In June 1777, a second law was passed (a Phase II),[†] on the ground that the prices fixed by the first law were "not adequate to the expense which will hereafter probably be incurred in procuring such articles."[46] A few months later, in September, the General Court of Massachusetts, convinced that the price-fixing measures

---

[†]Editor's Note: 'Phase II' refers to the second stage of President Nixon's multi-staged wage and price control program.

"have been very far from answering the salutary purposes for which they were intended" completely repealed both laws.[47]

Washington at Valley Forge

In Pennsylvania, where the main force of Washington's army was quartered in 1777, the situation was even worse. The legislature of that commonwealth decided to try a period of price control limited to those commodities needed for the use of the army. The theory was that this policy would reduce the expense of supplying the army and lighten the burden of the war upon the population. The result might have been anticipated by those with some knowledge of the trials and tribulations of other states. The prices of uncontrolled goods, mostly imported, rose to record heights. Most farmers kept back their produce refusing to sell at what they regarded as an unfair price. Some who had large families to take care of even secretly sold their food to the British who paid in gold.

After the disastrous winter at Valley Forge when Washington's army nearly starved to death (thanks largely to these well-intentioned but misdirected laws) the ill-fated experiment in price controls was finally ended. The Continental Congress on June 4, 1778, adopted the following resolution:

> "Whereas . . . it hath been found by experience that limitations upon the prices of commodities are not only ineffectual for the purposes proposed, but likewise productive of very evil consequences to the great detriment of the public service and grievous oppression of individuals . . . resolved, that it be recommended to the several states to repeal or suspend all laws or resolutions within the said states respectively limiting, regulating or restraining the Price of any Article, Manufacture or Commodity."[48]

One historian of the period tells us that after this date commissary agents were instructed "to give the current price . . . let it be what it may, rather than that the army should suffer, which you have to supply and the intended expedition be retarded for want of it." By the Fall of 1778 the army was fairly well-provided for as a direct result of this change in policy. The same historian goes on to say that "the flexibility in offering prices and successful purchasing in the country in 1778 procured needed winter supplies wanting in the previous year."[49]

The American economist, Pelatiah Webster, writing toward the end of the War of Independence in January, 1780, evaluted in a few succinct words the sporadic record of price and wage controls in the new United States. "As experiment is the surest proof of the natural effects of all speculations of this kind," he wrote, ". . . it is strange, it is marvelous to me, that any person of common discernment, who has been acquainted with all the above mentioned trials and effects, should entertain any idea of the expediency of trying any such methods again . . . Trade, if let alone, will ever make its own way best, and like an irresistible river, will ever run safest, do least mischief and do most good, suffered to run without obstruction in its own natural channel."[50]

V. THE FRENCH REVOLUTION

During the twenty months between May 1793 and December 1794, the Revolutionary Government of the new French Republic tried almost every experiment in wage and price controls which has been attempted before or since.

At the beginning of 1793, France found itself besieged by all the powers of Europe and blockaded by the British fleet. On the home front, her currency was rapidly falling in value and inflation was rampant. On the other hand, France was the richest agricultural country in Europe and the harvest of 1793 was to be particularly abundant.[51]

Her food problem in that year was not one of production but rather of distribution.[52] A constant series of decrees and regulations, each one designed to remedy the defects of the last, had the effect of leading the bread basket of Europe to the brink of starvation.

The Law of the Maximum

The first of these laws aimed at keeping prices down was passed by the Committee of Public Safety on May 3, 1793, together with a progressive tax on the rich and forced loans.[53] This first Law of the Maximum, as it was called, provided that the price of grain and flour in each district of France should be the average of local market prices which were in effect from January to May 1793. In addition, farmers were required to accept in payment the paper *assignats* at their face value, just as if they were coin.

Naturally many farmers kept their produce away from the markets since they were not allowed to ask a fair price for their goods in a time of rising inflation. Popular uprisings took place in several departments and by August of that year the May Law was generally regarded as a dead letter.

On September 11, 1793 a new plan, which might be called Phase II, was adopted by the National Convention: a uniform price for a long list of goods was set for the whole country, with allowances made for the cost of transportation. This plan too was soon discarded and the Law of September 29 was proclaimed (Phase III). The new system provided that prices should be fixed at the local rates of 1790 plus one-third.

In a little over a month, this plan too was clearly shown to be a failure and the Law of November 1 (Phase IV) was enacted. This latest attempt at regulating prices was more complicated than the previous phases. Prices were to be based upon those of 1790 at the place of production plus one-third plus a rate per league for transportation plus 5 per cent for the wholesaler and 10 per cent for the retailer. Local governments were given the right to compel farmers to bring their grain to markets and to sell it at the fixed price. By the use of the army and police, enough farmers were physically transported (with their grain) to marketplaces to enable the French people to survive the last months of 1793 and the first months of 1794.[54]

The revised system of price control was, of course, no more successful than previous attempts. One scholar has succinctly explained why:

"This scheme, judged from the point of view of modern experience, had two bad features. The first was the failure to guarantee the farmer a reasonable profit, and so encourage him to put more acres under cultivation and raise larger crops. Should his labors slacken and his crops become small, no amount of energy in insisting upon a fair distribution of the product would keep the people from going hungry. The scheme not only failed to encourage the farmer, it threatened him with ruin. His expenses for tools, draft animals and wages were steadily rising, but his profits were cut down, with the prospect of further losses every succeeding month."

"The second blunder was the obverse of this; it was the assumption that force could be used successfully with the largest body of producing workmen the country had. The agents utilized to apply the force, when the last links in the chain of authority were reached, would be the farmers themselves, for the communal officers were either farmers or men dependent upon them."[55]

A large black market grew up all over France in response to the government's repeated attempts to control the prices of foodstuffs. Butter, eggs and meat in particular, were sold in small quantities door-to-door, mainly to the rich.[56] It was impossible to control this contraband trade and the net effect was to insure that the wealthy had more than enough food while the poor were left to go hungry. In other words, the actual results of the Law of the Maximum were precisely the opposite of what was intended.

An Englishwoman living in Amiens wrote that "detachments of dragoons are obliged to scour the country to preserve us from famine." By the summer of 1794, demands were coming from all over the country for the immediate repeal of the Law. In some towns in the South the people were so badly fed that they were collapsing in the streets from lack of nourishment. The department of the Nord complained bitterly that their shortages all began just after the passage of the by now hated Law of the Maximum. "Before that time," they wrote to the Convention in Paris, "our markets were supplied, but as soon as we fixed the price of wheat and rye we saw no more of those grains. The other kinds not subject to the maximum were the only ones brought in. The deputies of the Convention ordered us to fix a maximum for all grains. We obeyed and henceforth grain of every sort disappeared from the markets. What is the inference? This, that the establishment of a maximum brings famine in the midst of abundance. What is the remedy? Abolish the maximum."[57]

The attempts of the French Republic to control the prices of food were clearly doomed; many areas of France did not wait for the national government to act but repealed the hated law by popular vote. Finally, in December 1794, the extremists in the Convention were defeated and the price control law was officially repealed. When Robespierre and his colleagues were being carried through the streets of Paris on their way to their executions, the mob jeered their last insult: "There goes the dirty Maximum."[58]

VI. THE FIRST WORLD WAR

With the outbreak of the First World War in 1914 the most wide-spread and extensive system of economic controls in history began to go into effect. Before the war was over all the major industrialized nations had enacted regulations governing production, distribution, profits, prices and in many cases, wages.

The U.K.

In Great Britain, the sudden and dramatic upsurge of government demands for supplies combined with almost immediate shortages caused by the German submarine fleet, drove prices far above pre-war levels. There were insistent demands, of course, for the government to 'do something.'

The new government regulations, however, led to a whole series of difficulties and produced many new problems. *The Spectator* pointed out that the dangers of government controls were double in character; they were both political and economic. Politically, too much power is concentrated in the hands of the government and the people become accustomed to relying upon government to accomplish goals which can best be done by the workings of individual initiative and the free market.[59] As prices are artificially kept down in times of increasing demand and diminishing supply, the only results are inconveniences and disappointments. People go to the shops expecting to find food available at the legal prices and go away disappointed.[60] Many people are also made to believe that high prices are caused by unseen manipulations which could be corrected by government manipulations.[61] They then ask for still stricter controls and yet more state interference.

Economically speaking, *The Spectator* and other journals pointed out, in times of increasing demands and decreasing supplies, high prices are necessary. They act as a rationing system, checking consumption and channeling goods into areas where they can be most productively used. Besides reducing waste, high prices act as a stimulant to production and importation. A free price system, in short, works to end a period of shortages and tends to solve economic problems. Government controls or rationing only act to prolong the shortages.[62] *The Fortnightly* warned that by restricting prices the government is "encouraging consumption, discouraging production and preparing disaster."[63] *The Saturday Review* declared that it is much easier to fix price ceilings than to make certain that there actually will be goods available at such prices. Once government fixes prices it is forced into the position of seeing to it that the owners of goods do not withhold them from sale and that manufacturers and farmers continue production. This amounts to nothing less than industrial conscription.[64] *The Nation* noted that without such conscription, a necessary corollary of government-fixed maximum prices set below the market rates, "a period of acute shortage, even of starvation, for the poor can be easily brought about."[65]

As *The Edinburgh Review* underscored, government regulation of the economy cannot be done without tying up the entire trade of a nation in official rules and red tape. Numerous boards and commissions must be appointed, countless clerks and supervisors employed, innumerable orders, rules and regulations must be issued. Perhaps worst of all it also "involves endless frauds, including the wholesale forgery of food tickets, together with a general lowering of the moral standards of the community."[66] *The Fortnightly Review* remarked dryly that a process which began with the promulgating of a few orders holding down prices ended by reaching a stage "when practially everything is controlled, and the greater the control the more complete the confusion and the greater the economic loss."[67]

After the war, one of the most respected journals in the world, *The Economist* of London, summed up succinctly the legacy of controls in Great Britain. "Why not let it alone? (It was) repeatedly said, in response to the shortsighted demand for control of prices, that price was less important than supply, and that if the State prevented prices from rising by artificial interference, it might cut off the supplies that high prices would attract . . . The State (nonetheless) interfered in every possible direction . . . The country now can view the results. On every side failure is visible and palpable. No single branch of trade which the government has touched shows a success."[68]

No controls in the U.S.?

The experience of the United States of America with economic regulation during the war was not very much different from that of Great Britain or indeed of other industralized nations. The economic historian, Simon Litman, noted that "government price fixing during the war was guided little by economic principles. It was not uniform either in its objects or in its methods feeling its way from case to case. It might be termed opportunist."[69]

Oddly enough, no statute authorizing over-all fixing of prices was enacted by the United States Government during the war. The War Industries Board derived such power as it had to set prices from the power granted to the President to place compulsory purchase orders with any manufacturer and the related power to set priorities. In 1917 the Food and Fuel Administration was given very wide powers over the prices of food and fuel products and later the War Industries Board set up a Price Fixing Committee to establish prices for goods other than food and fuels. Generally, it fixed prices at rather high levels permitting the low-cost producers in an industry to make huge profits.[70]

In theory, the Price Fixing Committee set prices by agreement with the industry concerned. Bernard Baruch, in his 1921 report to the President on the experience of government war-time economic controls, noted that "the bases in law for different regulations were varied, and in some cases doubtful." Mr. Baruch himself later pointed out that in fact most of the so-called 'voluntary agreements' were in fact imposed on industries under the threat of commandeering.[71]

Dr. Simon Litman summed up his study of the effects of price control in the United States in 1917-18 by concluding that "the fixing of a 'reasonable' price, when the supply of a commodity is not sufficient to meet the usual demand, cannot prevent hardships and dissatisfaction. Price-fixing alone does not solve the problem of keeping the poor provided with commodities; in fact, 'reasonable' prices may aggravate the situation by giving people of means an incentive and an opportunity to acquire ahead of their actual needs, thus leaving the less fortunate ones without any supply."[72]

Not a liberal policy

It would be fair to conclude that most American economists regarded the experiment with price controls in the First World War as having, at best, mixed results. Almost all students of the subject opposed their continuance in peacetime. *The American Economic Review*, in a special supplement published in March 1919, included an analysis of the possibilities of price-fixing in time of peace. "A general policy of price-fixing, however democratic the government that adopts it, is an illiberal rather than a liberal policy . . .," the author asserted. "If we adopt a general, undiscriminating policy of price-fixing as a part of a permanent peace program, we shall be going backward rather than forward; we shall be returning to a regime of authority and compulsion rather than going forward toward a regime of voluntary agreement among free citizens."[73]

Czechoslovakia

Price controls were attempted by one of the new democracies to emerge from World War I in the first years of peace with results similar to those predicted by British, American and other economists. A study of the Carnegie Endowment for International Peace on the economic and social history of the World War reported that "not only did the attempt of the Government (of Czechoslovakia) to reduce prices by official order fail — it was bound to fail according to the laws of political economy — but it had the effect of constantly driving prices and costs of production upwards."[74] In December of 1920, "the control of meat and fats was discontinued altogether and that of corn and flour restricted."[75] The author of this study concluded: "All this the people felt to be servitude rather than beneficent rule, so that even the most strenuous champions of economic control were compelled at length to capitulate."[76]

Russia

Although price controls seemed to have been something less than efficacious in democracies it might be expected that they would work better in a dictatorship. The case of Russia at this period provides an almost perfect laboratory. Prior to 1917, that vast country was ruled by a semifeudal despot and after November of that year it fell into the hands of the Bolsheviks. Under the Imperial Government, the bureaucracy issued contradictory and confusing regulations which only succeeded in bringing the economy to the brink of chaos. The enforcement of a consistent policy on prices was not possible mainly because the government itself violated its own rules. "The authorized agents of the Ministry of War" we are told, "bought up supplies for the army at prices much higher than those officially fixed."[77]

When the Bolsheviks seized power from the Social Democrats in November, they "abolished all freedom of trade and inaugurated a severe policy of fixed prices on all necessary articles of consumption. The peasants retaliated by refusing to sell their produce, whereupon the Soviet Government began its systematic campaign against the villages, which continued for about two years and ended with the complete defeat of the Bolsheviks."[78] An observer who visited Moscow in 1919 reported that "controlled prices do not, in fact, exist. They are merely issued as decrees to which no one pays the slightest attention."[79]

It might be thought that price-fixing in the two kinds of dictatorship in Russia was still not given a fair trial because both the Czar and the Communists presided over an essentially weak government ravaged by long years of war and hampered by the inherent problems of a backward nation. For a genuine test of what can be done by a firm dictatorship in a modern, industrialized nation one should examine events in Germany.

Germany

"The most comprehensive experiment in Europe in direct price-fixing," according to one scholar, "was that carried out by the German government subsequent to the outbreak of war in August, 1914." After discussing all of the many regulations designed to lower prices, he concludes that the Imperial Government was simply not effective in preventing a large increase in the cost of food.[80]

An English economist, writing in 1916, concluded that "the lesson from the German experiment in the State control of food prices is not that maximum prices must inevitably fail in all circumstances. All that can be definitely asserted is that in this outstanding instance, Germany, the organized State *par excellence*, showed itself unable to make maximum prices work to any sort of national advantage."[81]

Summary

The record of government attempts to control the economies of the industralized participants in the First World War, democracies and dictatorships, Allies and Central Powers, seems inescapable. A prominent Canadian economist having no control system at home to observe, examined the systems of price-fixing in Great Britain, France, Germany, the United States and Australia during this period. He came to the conclusion that, "the policy of fixing maximum prices . . . fails to accomplish the objects sought and it has a multitude of unforseen consequences which are frequently worse than the original evils."[82]

VII. THE SECOND WORLD WAR

A naive observer might have expected that at least one nation would have learned from the experience of 5,000 years when the Second World War broke out in 1939. None did, however, and all the major nations proceeded to set up machinery for government controls over a wide range of economic activities.

Due to the inherent nature of their social and political systems, some nations began the process earlier than others. Fascist Italy, for instance, moved toward government control over the economy as soon as Benito Mussolini was installed as Prime Minister and "Duce" in 1922.

Italy

On April 3, 1926, the Rocco Law of Corporations was promulgated under which 22 "Corporazione" were established, presided over by Mussolini. The Labor Charter of April 21, 1927, included a section (Article IX) which specifically allowed the government to intervene in all economic affairs. "State intervention in economic production," it declared, "takes place only when private initiative is lacking or insufficient, or when the state's political interests are at stake. Such intervention may take the form of controls, encouragement or direct management."[83]

The provisions of this law were soon put into effect in an attempt to stem the tide of the world-wide depression. Despite rigid price-fixing backed by a totalitarian regime, Italian prices and wages steadily declined and many businesses collapsed as the unemployment rolls swelled. Although the economy still floundered, government controls did have at least one major result; they gave Mussolini almost absolute control over the labor movement and slightly less control over industry and businesses.

Germany

In Nazi Germany, events took a similar course, except that economic controls were administered with far more ruthlessness. In May, 1933, shortly after the Nazis came to power, trade unions were suppressed and merged into a German labor front. The Law Regulating National Labor was enacted on January 20, 1934. Wages were determined by labor trustees, appointed by the Nazi-controlled Labor Front. Hitler was quite clear about his plans to keep wages low. "It has been the iron principle of National Socialist leadership," he announced, ". . . not to permit any rise in the hourly wage rates but to raise income solely by increase in performance."[84] In September, 1938, the four-year plan was launched under the direction of Hermann Goering. The purpose was to make Germany economically independent and ready for war. "Imports were reduced to a bare minimum (and) severe price and wage controls were introduced."[85]

An authoritative critique of the Third Reich's economic policy was given by Reichsmarschall Hermann Goering (who was responsible, among other things, for economic planning) while a prisoner of war in 1946. He told the war correspondent Henry J. Taylor that "Your America is doing many things in the economic field which we found out caused us so much trouble. You are trying to control people's wages and prices — people's work. If you do that you must control people's lives. And no country can do that part way. I tried it and failed. Nor can any country do it all the way either. I tried that too and it failed. You are no better planners than we. I should think your economists would read what happened here . . ."

"Will it be," he asked, "as it always has been that countries will not learn from the mistakes of others and will continue to make the mistakes of others all over again and again?"[86]

Canada

The Canadian war-time control system was the most comprehensive attempt at price freezing that any country, up to that time, had ever been subjected to:

> "It was a novel experiment, never before attempted in any democratic country; even the German 'price stop' of 1936 had been much less far-reaching . . ."[87]

The *Maximum Prices Regulations* of December 1, 1941 provided that no good or service could be sold at a price above that charged during the historical period September 15 to October 11, 1941. The price regulations were part of an overall economic mobilization program that included wage and salary controls, income and excess profits taxation, savings campaigns and a massive conservation program encouraging people to "eat it up", "wear it out", "make it do". Setting of production priorities, production directives, raw material allocation, distribution controls and selective service regulations were also part of the overall mobilization effort. In recognition of the fact that the price of imported goods could not be controlled, the government established a system of subsidies to enable it to freeze the domestic price of imported goods. (A similar stance was taken during 1974-1975 by the government of Canada with respect to the price of oil.)

The system of economy-wide controls that the government installed for the purpose of prosecuting the war effort was consciously designed to remove any semblance of market forces from the process of resource allocation. Canada actively encouraged inter-allied economic planning and the communal use of the raw materials available. In short, there was a total commitment to the war and virtually total sacrifice of personal economic freedoms.

"The government, with the overwhelming support of the people, was committed to an all-out war effort . . .

Reliance on a free price system would have required the government to keep continuously outbidding its citizens. The consequent rapid and accelerating rise in prices would have entailed acute hardship . . ."[88]

There is an element of self-contradiction in these two remarks. Surely, the very best test of the first of these statements would have been the government's reliance on people's free choice in the market place rather than on coercion as a means of carrying on the war. The second statement contradicts the first and clearly indicates that, by and large, the population would not have supported the war effort to the extent that it did, without the coercive measures adopted by government. Nevertheless, there was certainly wide-ranging support for the program and people were, it seems, willing to give up their economic freedoms in the short-run for the sake of freedom in the long-run.

As we have seen, mankind has a terrible tendency to forget and hence repeat historical experiences. Human beings also have a tendency to 'color' past experiences — the 'good old days' phenomenon being a good example of this sort of behavior. In looking back on the war years there seems to be an assumption that wage and price controls 'worked' — that they accomplished something that would not have occurred in their absence. It is certainly true that production controls 'worked' in the sense that large volumes of resources were devoted to the production of war *materiel.* It is not clear, however, that this redirection of resources was accomplished without the inflation that would have occurred had there been no controls.

An interesting test of the idea that controls reduced the inflation associated with the Second World War is provided by a comparison of that inflation with the inflation during the period of the First World War. The impression given by the cost of living indices reproduced in table 1 and chart 1 is that, overall, the control program adopted during the Second World War had the effect of preventing the surge in prices that was associated with the First World War. Notably, the controls did not keep prices from ultimately rising by about the same amount. There is reason to believe, however, that there was much more inflation during the Second World War than is suggested by the price index.

> "No matter how rigidly prices were held in check, costs tended to creep up . . . The major attack on this problem was along the lines of simplification and standardization in both production and distribution . . . reducing the number of varieties or models, cutting out frills, minimizing the use of scarce materials. . . every class of industry was affected."[89]

In other words there was a conscious effort to reduce the quality of every commodity that Canadians bought, to prevent the quoted prices from 'creeping up'. Since it is clear that quality degradation was used to cut costs, what are we to make of the 'reported' price index?

Table I — Cost of Living
1935-1939=100

Year	Cost of Living	World War I Index	Year	Cost of Living	World War II Index
1913	79.5	100	1939	101.5	100
1914	80.0	101	1940	105.6	104
1915	81.4	102	1941	111.7	110
1916	88.1	111	1942	117.2	115
1917	104.3	131	1943	119.2	117
1918	118.1	149	1944	119.8	118
1919	129.8	163	1945	120.4	119
1920	150.4	189	1946	124.5	123
1921	132.3	166	1947	136.3	134
1922	121.1	152	1948	155.7	153
1923	121.5	153	1949	161.6	159

Source: M.C. Urquhart ed., *Historical Statistics of Canada*, 1965, p. 304, Series J139-140.

"It would be impossible to give any quantitative expression to the savings in man-power, materials or money which these orders achieved, but they were very considerable and undoubtedly were of major importance in enabling the Board . . . to 'hold the line' effectively."[90]

Accordingly, all that we can say for sure is that the official statistics for the rate of inflation during the Second World War represent a 'considerable' underestimate of the true inflation situation. Accordingly, the straight-forward comparison of the official statistics is not a totally meaningful exercise. In spite of this, the statistics indicate that after the 'smoke had cleared', prices had risen by about the same amount over both war periods. We must therefore, seriously question whether the controls did indeed have much effect. In any event, it cannot simply be accepted that, even under those stringent war-time conditions, controls were successful.[91]

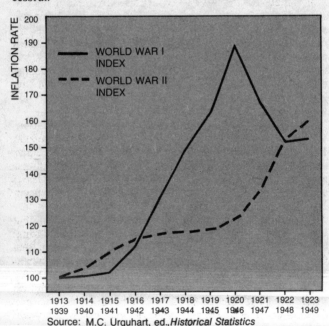

Source: M.C. Urquhart, ed.,*Historical Statistics of Canada,* 1965, p. 304. Series J139-146.

U.S.

When the United States entered World War II, the Roosevelt Administration delayed imposing price and wage controls for almost two years. This reluctance may well have been stimulated by the example of Germany and Italy; restrictions on personal freedom were not altogether welcome in the midst of an all-out war in defense of freedom. From January 1941, until October 1942, the government attempted to restrain the inevitable rise in both prices and wages by 'voluntary' controls and moral persuasion. During that period, wholesale prices rose almost 24 per cent and consumer prices over 18 per cent. With the establishment of the Office of Price Administration and the imposition of strict controls, however, consumer prices rose 8.7 per cent from October 1942 to August 1945. Price and wage controls were relatively effective during the Second World War largely because of the strong patriotic feeling which supported any government action that seemed to bring the end of the war nearer. Even so, hourly wage rates in manufacturing rose 14.7 per cent in that same 35 month period.[92] The rise in prices was not as steep because some manufacturers lowered the quality of goods while not raising the official selling price and many persons engaged in the black market, paying very high prices to get what they wanted when they wanted it.

After the war was over, however, the pent-up inflation burst and the controls broke down completely. From August 1945 to November 1946 wholesale prices rose over 32 per cent and consumer prices almost 18 per cent.[93] It is entirely possible, therefore, that the end result would have been almost the same by the year 1946 if controls had never been introduced in the first place.

Much the same series of events occurred when the United States next imposed price and wage controls during the Korean War. In June 1950, when the war began, the Consumer Price Index stood at 177.8. Half a year later, when controls went into effect the Index was at the level of 184.7 In September of 1952 when that freeze ended, the Consumer Price Index had reached 191.1. It would seem clear from the experience of Korean War controls that price and wage restraints, in the long run, have little effect in controlling inflation. The effects, of course, are largely negative. Thousands of bureaucrats spend hundreds of thousands of man-hours doing essentially non-productive work. In addition, the economy is distorted in numerous ways as workers, businessmen, and consumers devote their energies to getting around controls.

And the U.K. too . . .

Finally, to end this brief survey of 5,000 years of experience with wage and price controls, mention must be made of the U.K.'s controls during the Second World War. On September 3, 1939, when Prime Minister Neville Chamberlain broadcast the news that Britain was at war with Germany he commented: "It is evil things we shall be fighting against, brute force, bad faith, injustice, oppression and persecution."[94]

Inevitably, the mobilization and organization of the British people to enable Winston Churchill's war-time Coalition Government to pursue the war aim to the bitter end involved the central government taking upon itself almost limitless powers. According to the authors of the Civil History of Britain during the Second World War: "The year 1941 was certainly a watershed in the conduct of the war, producing firm policies of taxation, of free and forced saving, of price control, of rationing and control of civilian supplies, together with exhaustive discussions of wages policy."[95]

As the war neared its conclusion, so the debate continued on the best way for the smooth and orderly demobilization of the war-time economy, and the future of controls over labour, raw materials, finished products, prices and consumption. Following the election of Clement Attlee's Labour Government, his Chancellor of the Exchequer, Sir Stafford Cripps, instituted a policy of wage and dividend restraint, which, as Professor Parkin notes in the next chapter "was based on persuasion and voluntary compliance." "It must be borne in mind, however," Parkin comments "that throughout this period an elaborate system of points rationing, licencing and other war-time controls remained in force. These controls, in effect, temporarily replaced the resource allocating function normally performed by changes in prices and wages."

In 1952, the then Chairman of Lloyds Bank in England put the results of controls over the British economy in clear perspective. "There cannot really be any dispute," he wrote, "about the superior *efficiency* of a properly working price system . . . Rationing and controls are merely methods of *organizing* scarcity; the price system automatically works toward *overcoming scarcity.* If a commodity is in short supply, a rise in its price does not merely reduce demand but will also stimulate an increase in its supply. In this, the price system stands in direct contrast with rationing and controls, which tend to make it less profitable or less attractive in other ways, to engage in essential production than to produce the inessentials which are left uncontrolled."[96]

As Professor Parkin concludes in his study, the existence of controls has certainly contributed to "Britain's last twenty-five years of slide into economic and social chaos." One should add, this has happened largely, if not entirely, because of the continuation of the policies of planning, control and growing government intervention in the economy; policies which were widely endorsed and probably inevitable in the crucible of war-time conditions, but which have become obviously more and more disastrously redundant in peace-time society in Britain. Hence, the utter irony of the saying, "Great Britain won the war but lost the peace."

Notes

[1]Jewkes, John, *The New Ordeal by Planning*, London, 1967, *passim.*

[2]Lacy, Mary G., "Food Control During Forty-six Centuries: A Contribution to the History of Price Fixing," *Scientific Monthly*, June, 1923, p. 623-7. Much of the discussion of the early historical period is drawn from this excellent article.

[3]Olds, Irving S., *The Price of Price Controls*, Irvington-on-Hudson, N.Y., 1952, p. 4.

[4]Chen, Huan-Chang *The Economic Principles of Confucius and His School*, N.Y., 1911.

[5]*Ibid.*

[6]Lysias, "Against the Grain Dealers", *Eight Orations of Lysias* (edited by Morris Morgan), Boston, 1895, p. 89-103. For a translation, see Botsford, G. and Sihler, S., *Hellenic Civilization*, N.Y., 1915, p. 426-430.

[7]Lacy, *op. cit.*, p. 627-29.

[8]This account is based largely on that provided by H. Michell, "The Edict of Diocletian: A Study of Price Fixing in the Roman Empire", *The Canadian Journal of Economics and Political Science*, February 1947, p. 1-12.

[9]*Ibid.*, p. 2.

[10]*Ibid.*, p. 1

[11]*Ibid.*, p. 3.

[12]*Ibid.*, p. 5.

[13]It is also clear that the Edict was intended to reduce the costs of maintaining the army. ". . . an inspection of the items of the Edict will reveal that a majority of the maximum prices ordered refer to articles that enter largely into military stores", Michell, p. 8.

[14]Michell, p. 8.

[15]Lactantius, L.C.F., *A Relation of the Death of the Primitive Persecutors* (translated by Gilbert Burnet), Amsterdam, 1687, p. 67-8.

[16]Michell, p. 11.

[17]Michell, p. 12.

[18]Gibbon, Edward, *The History of the Decline and Fall of the Roman Empire*, N.Y., 1906, vol. 4, p. 111-12.

[19]Ashley, W.J., *English Economic History*, London, 1923-5, vol. 1, part 1, p. 181.

[20]*Ibid.*, p. 191.

[21]Litman, Simon, *Prices and Price Control in Great Britain and the United States During the World War*, New York, 1920, p. 6.

[22]Ashley, *op. cit.*, p. 30.

[23]Holdsworth, William, *A History of English Law*, London, 1922-26, vol. 2, p. 377.

[24]Fiske, John, *The Unseen World and Other Essays*, Boston, 1904, p. 20.

[25]Hunter, William, *Annals of Rural Bengal*, London, 1897, p. 7.

[26]*Extrait des Registres du Conseil Superieur de Quebec.* From Canadian Archives, Collection Moreau St. Mery, VI, 55-58, 21 fevrier, 1683.

[27]Canadian Archives, CIIA, XLIX, 183-192. Written about 1727.

[28]Canadian Archives, Collection Moreau St. Mery, XI, 332-334. *Memoire du Roy.*

[29]*Reglement du Conseil Superieur de Quebec,* 30 mars 1701. From Canadian Archives, Collection Moreau St. Mery, VIII, Pt. 2, p. 211-214.

[30]*Memoire sur le commerce de l'isle Royale joint a la lettre de Monsieur Prevost.* Canadian Archives, CIIB, XXXIII, 124.

[31]*Exposition du prix des denrees en Canada: Observations.* Canadian Archives, CIIE, X, p. 256-258.

[32]Weeden, William, *Economic and Social History of New England, 1620-1789,* New York, 1890, vol. 1, p. 99.

[33]*Ibid.*

[34]Winthrop, John, *The History of New England from 1630-1649,* Boston, 1825, vol. 1, p. 116.

[35]Weeden, *loc.cit.*

[36]*Ibid.,* p. 98.

[37]Connecticut, Bureau of Labor Statistics, *Third Annual Report for the Year Ending November 30, 1887,* Hartford, 1887, p. 225.

[38]Alvord, Clarence, *The Illinois Country, 1673-1818,* Springfield, Ill., 1920, p. 106-08.

[39]Bezanson, Anne, *Prices and Inflation During the American Revolution,* Philadelphia, 1951, p. 35.

[40]Bolles, Albert, *The Financial History of the United States,* New York, 1884, vol. 1, p. 160.

[41]*Connecticut, Public Records of the State,* Hartford, 1894-1922, vol. 1, p. 62.

[42]*Ibid.,* p. 366.

[43]Sumner, William Graham, *The Financier and the Finances of the American Revolution,* New York, 1891, vol. 1, p. 65.

[44]*Ibid.,* p. 66.

[45]Harlow, Ralph, *Economic Conditions in Massachusetts During the American Revolution,* Cambridge, Mass., 1918, p. 167.

[46]*Ibid.*

[47]*Ibid.*

[48]*Journals of the Continental Congress,* New York, 1908, vol. 21, p. 569.

[49]Bezanson, *op. cit.,* p. 86.

[50]Webster, Pelatiah, *Political Essays,* Philadelphia, 1791, p. 65-66.

[51]Litman, *op. cit.,* p. 7.

[52]Bourne, Henry, "Food Control and Price-Fixing in Revolutionary France," *The Journal of Political Economy,* February 1919, p. 75.

[53]Litman, *op. cit.,* p. 6.

[54]Bourne, Henry, "Maximum Prices in France," *American Historical Review,* October 1917, p. 112.

[55]Bourne, *Journal of Political Economy, op. cit.,* p. 88.

[56]Bourne, *American Historical Review, loc. cit.*

[57]Bourne, *Journal of Political Economy, op. cit.,* p. 93.

[58]Bourne, *Journal of Political Economy,* March 1919, p. 208.

[59]*The Spectator,* January 23, 1917, p. 692.

[60]*Ibid.*, March 31, 1917, p. 382.

[61]Shadwell, A., "Food Prices and Food Supply," *The Nineteenth Century and After*, April 1917, p. 736.

[62]*The Spectator*, February 6, 1915, p. 181.

[63]*Fortnightly Review*, March 1917, p. 438.

[64]*The Saturday Review*, September 9, 1917, p. 242.

[65]*The Nation*, January 2, 1917.

[66]*The Edinburgh Review*, July 1917, p. 50.

[67]*Fortnightly Review*, January 1918, p. 45.

[68]*The Economist*, vol. 89, September 6, 1919, p. 387-88.

[69]Litman, *op. cit.*, p. 318.

[70]Hensel, Struve and McClung, Richard, "Profit Limitation Controls Prior to the Present War," *Law and Contemporary Problems*, Duke University, Autumn 1943, p. 195.

[71]*Ibid.*, p. 196.

[72]*Ibid.*, p. 319.

[73]Carver, T.N., "The Possibilities of Price Fixing in Time of Peace," *American Economic Review*, March 1919, p. 247.

[74]Rasin, Alois, *Financial Policy of Czechoslovakia During the First Year of its History*, N.Y., 1923 (Carnegie Endowment for International Peace, Division of Economics and History, Economic and Social History of the World War), p. 15.

[75]*Ibid.*, p. 77.

[76]*Ibid.*, p. 153.

[77]Leites, Kussiel, *Recent Economic Developments in Russia*, (edited by Harald Westergaard), N.Y., 1922, p. 47.

[78]*Ibid.*, p. 115.

[79]Turin, S.P., "Market Prices and Controlled Prices of Food in Moscow," *Royal Statistical Society Journal*, May 1920, p. 478-9.

[80]Wilkinson, H.L., *State Regulation of Prices in Australia: A Treatise on Price Fixing and State Socialism*, Melbourne, 1917, p. 106-116.

[81]Hilton, John, "Germany's Food Problem and its 'Kontrolle' ", *Nineteenth Century and After*, January 1916, p. 29.

[82]Clark, W.C., *Should Maximum Prices be Fixed?* (Queen's University, Departments of History and Political and Economic Science, Bulletin 27), Kingston, Ontario, 1918, p. 25.

[83]Clough, Shepard and Saladino, Salvatore, *A History of Modern Italy*, N.Y., 1968, p. 467.

[84]Shirer, William, *The Rise and Fall of the Third Reich*, New York, 1960, p. 263.

[85]*Ibid.*, p. 261.

[86]Harper, F.A., *Stand-By Controls*, Irvington-on-Hudson, N.Y., 1953, p. 20.

[87]Taylor, K.W., Canadian War-time Price Controls, 1941-6, *Canadian Journal of Economics and Political Science*, February 1947, p. 87. The present account draws heavily from this source.

[88]*Ibid.*, p. 85.

[89] *Ibid.*, p. 91.

[90] *Ibid.*, p. 92.

[91] In addition to these observations, there is also the very familiar antecdotal evidence of black marketing, ration coupon skullduggery, etc., all of which indicates that official statistics would have underestimated the true 'market' price of commodities.

[92] U.S. Department of Labor, Bureau of Labor Statistics, *Handbook of Labor Statistics*, 1947 edition, Bulletin 916, Washington, D.C., 1948, p. 107-108, 127-28, and 54; and *Monthly Labor Review*, November 1943, p. 879; November 1945, p. 1045; and November 1947, p. 609.

[93] *Ibid.*

[94] David Thomson, *England in the Twentieth Century*, Penguin Books, 1965, page 209.

[95] W.K. Hancock and M.M. Gowing, *British War Economy*, His Majesty's Stationery Office, London, 1949, page 152.

[96] *Newsweek*, September 8, 1952, page 78.

The Post-War Record

Wage and Price Controls: The Lessons From Britain

MICHAEL PARKIN

Professor of Economics
University of Western Ontario

THE AUTHOR

Michael Parkin was born in Yorkshire, England in 1939 and in 1963 was graduated from the University of Leicester. Until fall 1975, when he moved to Canada, he was Professor of Economics at the University of Manchester. Currently, he is Professor of Economics at the University of Western Ontario.

Professor Parkin's scholarly publications are numerous and include on the subject of inflation alone: *Incomes Policy and Inflation*, edited by M. Parkin and M.T. Sumner, University of Toronto Press, 1973; *Inflation in the World Economy*, University of Toronto Press, 1976; and "Inflation: A Survey" (with David Laidler), *Economic Journal*, December, 1975.

The Post-War Record

Wage and Price Controls: The Lessons From Britain

MICHAEL PARKIN

Professor of Economics
University of Western Ontario

I. INTRODUCTION

When Prime Minister Trudeau introduced Canada's current *Attack on Inflation*,[1] in October 1975† with a program of direct controls on wages and prices as its centrepiece, he made yet one more move in the direction of rejecting workable and potentially successful economic policies based on careful scientific analysis and of embracing policies based on ignorance, prejudice and instinctive reaction. It is an increasingly common view that the simultaneous pursuit of high and stable employment and stable prices via Keynesian-inspired economic policies is inconsistent with traditional free collective bargaining and market determination of prices. It is a popular view that 'new' prices and incomes policies must be adopted if the twin objectives of high and stable employment and stable prices are to be simultaneously achieved. In fact, nothing could be further from the truth. Rather, the so-called 'new' policies are the oldest[2] and crudest best likened to medieval medicine, based on ignorance and misunderstanding of the fundamental processes at work and more likely to kill the patient than to cure him.

†Editor's Note: Curiously, but surely not without significance, the same title as Harold Wilson's program launched in the U.K., August 1975.

Understanding inflation

It was not until relatively recently in the long sweep of human history, in the seventeenth and eighteenth centuries,[3] that the principles governing the determination of the general level of prices were made clear. The insights of Bodin and Hume and the refinements which have followed, through the work and writings of Irving Fisher, Wicksell, Keynes and modern monetary theorists such as Milton Friedman, are critical for understanding and influencing the fundamental monetary forces which determine the general level of prices, the rate of inflation and the general level of output and employment. In their way, these insights are as important as those of Newton and the subsequent refinements of his ideas for an understanding of gravity and the fundamental laws governing the behavior of physical matter. The fruits of this analysis and their implications for the control of inflation are set out by David Laidler in a subsequent study, in which it is shown that there does exist a coherent and workable, though inevitably non-painless, cure for Canada's current inflationary ills.

This study has the more negative, though vitally important task, of analyzing the effects of wage-price controls and of showing that, whatever their superficial attractiveness, they simply do not work. *They do not control inflation.* At best, they are evaded by the skilful use of legal and financial talent — talent which is scarce and could, more importantly should, be put to productive use. At worst, they distort the allocation of scarce economic resources, they produce arbitrary and in general unjust redistributions of income, they generate a deterioration in industrial relations and they engender a disregard for the rule of law. These are strong claims and cannot simply be made by assertion. Nor can they be justified by *a priori* argument. They must be demonstrated by hard evidence.

The British disease

Fortunately for Canada, whilst the present controls are the first such comprehensive program in peacetime, other than the voluntary restraint of 1969, other countries have pursued such policies extensively and have generated experience from which we can learn. Sad to say, experiments with the 'new' policies of wage and price controls have a long and checkered history. Robert Schuettinger, in a paper in this series, provides a short but devastating survey of these experiences. Much hard evidence is also available from recent and probably more relevant policy mistakes in the United Kingdom.

This experience is pertinent for Canada today for two key reasons. First, it is extensive, well-documented, and has been closely studied. Second, Canada in 1976 has, despite many obvious differences, a great deal in common with the United Kingdom. Like Britain, it has a political process which despite party labels, tends to produce governments either inclined or committed to intervene in people's affairs and to expand the government sector. It has labour unions which are apparently short-sighted and which consequently do not act in their own long-term self-interest. It has a large volume of, and dependence on, international trade and investment. Thus Canada has a great deal of value to learn from the mistakes of Britain's past twenty-five years of slide into economic and social chaos. *If the lesson is ignored*, Canada is well set on that same path. *If it is learned*, there is ample time to reverse the present trends and move this country to a path of unparalleled enlightenment and prosperity. The choice is simple, but the lesson apparently is hard to learn.

It is the purpose of this paper to try to spell out the lesson. It focuses solely on the United Kingdom's experience with wage-price controls since 1945. The study has three main sections. First, it examines Britain's post-war inflation record and describes the various episodes of controls. Second, it compares the performance of inflation in 'controls on' and 'controls off' periods and assesses the impact of controls on the pace of inflation. Third, it examines the side-effects of controls.

Chart 1 — United Kingdom Inflation, 1945-1975
(Retail Prices)

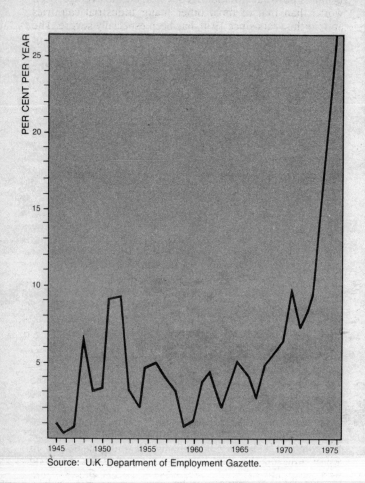

Source: U.K. Department of Employment Gazette.

II. INFLATION AND CONTROLS: THE BRITISH POST-WAR HISTORY

Britain's post-war inflation record has, on the average, been worse than that of most other major industrial countries and, in the years since 1970, has been especially severe. The full post-war record, as measured by the rate of inflation of retail (consumers') prices is set out in Chart 1. Three things stand out in this chart. First, with the exception of 1948, the Korean war years 1951-2 and the years since 1969, inflation has never been really severe and has uniformly been below 5 per cent per annum. Second, there has been, until recently, a pronounced and rather regular cycle with a duration of approximately four years. Third, there is no single discernible trend but rather two distinct sub-trends: the 1950's during which, measuring from trough to trough to avoid the distortion of the Korean War, the trend was clearly downwards, while in the 1960's and 1970's the price trend has been strongly upwards and explosively so in the final years.

Against this background of the ebbs and flows of the inflation tide, let us now briefly describe chronologically, the various episodes of 'prices and incomes policies'. Eleven distinct episodes can be identified, many of them consecutive.

Episode one — the Cripps-TUC co-op

The first ran from 1948 to 1950, and its chief feature was an impressive and widely-respected appeal by Sir Stafford Cripps, (the then Chancellor of the Exchequer), to the Trades Union Congress (TUC) for wage restraint and to the Federation of British Industry for dividend restraint. The episode ended in October 1950 with a vote by the TUC to abandon wage restraint. There were no statutory agencies set up to implement Cripps' policy and no announced 'norms' or guidelines. The entire program was based on persuasion and voluntary compliance. It must be borne in mind, however, that throughout this period, an elaborate system of points rationing, licencing and other wartime controls remained in force. These controls, in effect, temporarily replaced the resource allocating function normally performed by changes in prices and wages.

Episode two — mild rebuff

The second episode covered one year only, 1956, and was milder than either its predecessor or successors. It amounted to repeated requests by the then Conservative government for wage restraint and repeated refusals by the unions to cooperate.

Episode three — the pay pause

Episode three was initiated at the height of a balance-of-payments crisis in the summer of 1961 and was a request by the Conservative Government for a temporary wage freeze (or 'pay pause' as it was called). Again there was no enforcing agency and compliance was voluntary.

Episode four — the guiding light

The next episode was a direct extension of the previous one and was an attempt to make the relaxation of the 1961 wage freeze as orderly as possible. It specified a set of 'guiding lights' for wage and price rises based on the assumption that productivity would grow at 2.5 per cent per annum. The 'guiding light' for wages was to be a rise of 2 to 2.5 per cent per annum and for prices nil. Again these 'norms' were voluntary but for the first time an agency (the National Incomes Commission) was established to monitor and encourage compliance. However, the unions adopted a position of non-cooperation with this agency. The 2.5 per cent (maximum) 'guiding light' for wages was adjusted to 3.5 per cent in 1963 and by the time of the 1964 General Election (October) the policy was abandoned.

Episode five — accord

That election saw the return of a Labour Government after thirteen years of Conservative rule and, in consequence, a revival of cooperation between government and organized labour. By the middle of 1965, the new government was able to sign with the Trade Unions and the employers federation (the Confederation of British Industry) a *Joint Statement of Intent on Productivity, Prices and Incomes*, which set down a voluntary guideline of 3 to 3.5 per cent per annum for wage increases, rules for permissible price increases, and criteria for exceptions. It also established a National Board for Prices and Incomes. This episode of policy lasted until mid-1966.

Episode six — Labour — first forced freeze

The next episode was the first British attempt (and this by a Labour government) to impose *statutory* limits on wage and price increases with penalties (fines) for non-compliance and provision for 'roll-backs'. For the first six months, July to December 1966, there was a total wage freeze and to mid-1967 a further period of 'severe restraint'.

Episode seven — rule by exception

Episode seven was a mild relaxation of its predecessor. The force of the law still lay behind the guidelines, but more 'exceptional cases' were permitted to take pay increases above the 'norm'.

Episode eight — controls for a decade

The next episode was, in effect, the phasing out of the previous restraint. A White Paper published in April 1968, *Productivity, Prices and Incomes in 1968 and 1969*, reverted to a 3.5 per cent per annum norm for wage increases but made exceptions, both for 'lower paid' workers and in cases of 'productivity agreements'. These turned out to produce loopholes through which a blindfolded man could drive a bus and in effect were the method whereby the policy was gradually abandoned. The maximum permissible normal wage increase was raised from 3.5 to 4.5 per cent at the end of 1969 and the policy finally ended with the election of the new Conservative Government in June 1970. This also ended almost ten unbroken years of some form or other of wage and price controls.

Episode nine — Tory phased-freeze

Controls were reactivated by Edward Heath's Conservative Government in November 1972 in a three-stage statutory program. Stage I was a three month total freeze (similar to that imposed by President Nixon in 1971); Stage II a flat £1 per week plus 4 per cent to last six months; Stage III, a norm of 7 per cent plus partial indexation. Stage III was finally abandoned in a bitter conflict between the government and the coal miners which led to British industry being put on the three-day week and ended in the defeat of the Heath Government in February 1974.

Episode ten — Labour's social contract

The new Labour Government of Harold Wilson which emerged from the wreckage entered into a 'social contract' or voluntary incomes policy, with the unions, a contract described as 'not worth the paper on which it was not written' which pledged the government to deliver high employment and more sustained *real* income in return for the unions delivering moderation in *money* wage claims.

Episode eleven — *Attack on Inflation*

The final episode started in July 1975 and is still in force. This places statutory obligations on employers to limit pay increases to £6 per week (about 12 per cent of the average weekly wage) and to limit price rises to ensure that margins do not increase.

With all this vast variety and extent of experience, it should be possible to discover whether or not controls do have any effect on inflation and also to establish what side effects they have. We now turn to that task.

III. THE EFFECTS OF CONTROLS ON THE PACE OF INFLATION

Isolating the effects controls have had on the pace of inflation in the United Kingdom is no easy matter. The rate of inflation is subject to influences from many sources and it is necessary to assess what these influences are in order to remove their effect from our analysis and establish the separate and independent influence of wage-price controls.

As a preliminary to that analysis it is instructive to see how Britain's record of inflation lines up with its experience with controls. This is done in Chart 2 which repeats the course of inflation shown in Chart 1 and superimposes as shaded areas the various episodes of wage-price controls. What is striking about this chart is the lack of any systematic tendency for controls to be associated with a reduction in inflation. Indeed, in broad terms, the reverse is true. As controls have become more severe (with statutory controls replacing voluntary guidelines) and more prolonged, so the pace of inflation has accelerated.

Chart 2 — Inflation and Controls, United Kingdom 1945-1975

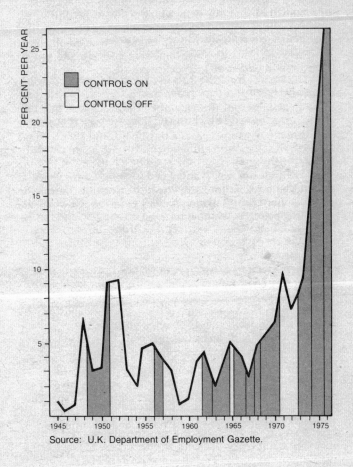

Source: U.K. Department of Employment Gazette.

Of course, to a large extent, this reflects causation running from inflation to controls. As inflation becomes more serious so it brings in its wake an increasing clamour for the government to 'do something' and, in view of their primitive appeal, controls are the natural measures to create the impression of government action. Few would want to deny that inflation leads to controls: but do controls lead to the moderation of inflation?

The answer from the facts portrayed in Chart 2 must be a qualified "no". It is true that in the *early phases* of episodes (1), (3) and (6) and throughout episodes (2) and (5), the rate of inflation did fall. However, it is also clear that in the *later phases* of episodes (1), (3) and (6) and in all other episodes of controls, the inflation rate continued to climb. It is noteworthy that, with the exception of 1956, the rate of U.K. inflation was *higher* at the end of each control episode than it had been at the beginning of the episode. However, we must qualify, with a caution, the conclusion that controls do not help to reduce inflation. Could it be that the forces making for inflation were on a strong upward trend, especially throughout the 1960's and that, bad though Britain's inflation record was over this period, in the absence of controls it would have been much worse? If we are to assess properly the contribution of the controls, we cannot dodge that question.

To answer this question it is necessary to establish what have been the main causes of inflation in postwar Britain and, in the light of these factors to predict the course that inflation would have taken in the absence of controls and then to measure the separate and independent effects of the controls.

What then have been the main sources of Britain's postwar inflation? This, of course, has been and continues to be a controversial question and one on which a great deal has been written — much by the present author.[4] It is also though a question on which a stronger consensus is beginning to emerge as the facts become clearer. The two broad opposing views on the question may be labelled: 'wage-push' and 'monetary-pull'.

Wage-push inflation

The wage-push view takes as its starting point factors which directly determine the rate of wage inflation. The central precondition for the wage-push analysis of inflation is the notion that, in an economy which uses Keynesian aggregate demand management techniques to maintain full employment, the demand for labour in aggregate will be almost independent of the level of money wages since any wage level will be validated by the actions of the government and central bank. Trade unions, behaving in the absence of constraints on employment will set wages in order primarily to achieve what they regard as fair wages. Concern with justice in the distribution of wages will ensure that any badly out-of-line high wage settlement in a particular sector of the economy will quickly transmit itself to other sectors, thereby preserving the general structure of relative wages but raising their overall level. With wages determined in this manner and with productivity growth determined by longer-term factors, unit costs and hence prices will inflate in line with the initiating behaviour of wages. Monetary and fiscal policy will accommodate and validate the inflation in order to ensure that real output does not fall and too much unemployment emerge. Further, if the inflation gets too far out of line with inflation in other countries, then, from time to time, the exchange rate will have to be depreciated.

Monetary-pull inflation

The alternative 'monetary-pull' view takes as its starting point an analysis of the socio-political factors which lead to the printing of an excessive supply of money relative to the demand for it. The central ingredients in this analysis are that vote-seeking politicians believe (rightly apparently) that, by increasing government expenditure on social programs, subsidies and the like, and by holding down interest rates, especially in the housing sector, they can improve their electoral chances. The result of such behaviour is an excessive rate of money creation to pay for the programs.

Excessive money supply leads first (with a variable time lag but a lag of between one and two years) to an increase in the demand for goods and labour services. With a further (variable) time lag of up to a year, this excess demand leads to faster rises in wages and prices. Further, because the prices of some groups are the costs of others, an interactive spiral between wages and prices is set up. The more persistent is the inflationary money creation process, the more will firms and unions come to expect its continuance and the faster will wages and prices rise simply in anticipation of what others are likely to do. If the resulting inflation is faster than in other countries, the exchange rate will eventually have to be depreciated. When this happens inflation will be given a further upward thrust, the magnitude of which will be determined by the country's dependence on imported goods.

What does cause inflation?

Having said what the two most popular views of inflationary forces are we must now decide which of them is correct. To do this we have to examine what actually happened in the United Kingdom and compare what actually happened to what these two theories would have predicted. First, let's consider what the theories would have predicted about the relationship between the rate of money creation and the rate of inflation.

According to the wage-push view the pressure for increases in wages produces, via cost increases, increases in prices. Increasing prices then produce pressure for increases in the money supply. Accordingly, if the wage-push theory is correct we expect to find that on average changes in wage growth and inflation precede, by a short interval, changes in monetary growth.

The monetary-pull view, on the other hand, maintains that a high rate of money creation is the cause of the inflation. Hence, if the monetary-pull view is correct we would expect to find that changes in the rate of inflation occur two or three years after a change in the rate of money creation.

The second relationship that we must analyze is that between changes in wages and the factors that are supposed to cause the changes.

From the point of view of the 'wage-push' theory, changes in wages represent a struggle for 'the income pie' and are only vaguely related to the demand for and supply of labour on the one hand and to inflation expectations on the other. If this view is correct, the rate of change in wages, on the whole, should be observed to adjust largely independently of labour market conditions and inflation expectations and respond, instead, to a whole variety of socio-psychological factors. If the 'monetary-pull' view is correct, wages should be seen to respond primarily to market forces — i.e. the supply of and demand for labour — and inflation expectations.

Chart 3 — Inflation Rate and Growth of Money Stock, United Kingdom 1964-1974

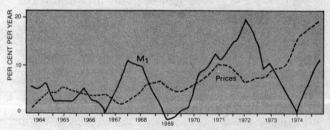

Source: Reproduced from "Where is Britain's Inflation Going?" *Lloyds Bank Review*, July 1975, No. 117.

We now have two predictions from each of the views of inflation. To determine which one of the theories is correct we must compare the predictions to what has actually happened. Let us look first at the relationship between money and inflation which Chart 3 illustrates. It shows the rate of inflation and the rate of growth of the money supply[5] on a quarterly frequency from the beginning of 1964.[6] Casual inspection of the chart does not reveal any strong correlation between money supply growth and inflation. However, more careful inspection reveals there to be a strong correlation between the rate of monetary expansion and the rate of inflation some three years later. There is no similarly strong correlation in the opposite direction. That is, there is no strong tendency for the rate of growth of money to lag behind inflation as is predicted by the 'wage-push' theory.

In terms of the cycles, these regularities can be seen most clearly in the latter part of the period depicted in the chart. The buildup of the money supply growth rate in 1967 and the U.K. devaluation of the pound of that year can be seen to have generated the inflation takeoff in 1969-70 and the even more dramatic buildup in the money supply growth rate from mid-1969 to mid-1972 as having brought the 1972 onwards inflation explosion. The reductions in the rate of inflation in 1969 and 1971-72 are equally clearly associated with earlier reductions in the rate of growth of the money supply in 1966 and 1968-69 respectively.

Thus, on the basis of this evidence, it appears that the 'monetary-pull' view is the correct explanation of Britain's inflation. It is also clear that the monetary forces making for faster inflation were in fact on the increase on the average through the later 1960's and 1970's. Hence, simply observing that inflation increased despite the presence of wage-price controls, does not lead to the inference that such controls were useless. We must examine whether, with controls in force, inflation was worse or better than it otherwise would have been. To do that within the framework of the relationship between money and inflation is not easy since that relationship is never exact and is subject to variable time lags. It turns out to be more fruitful to proceed by way of an analysis of the other relationship predicted by the 'monetary-pull' view and denied by the 'wage-push' view, that is the relationship between wages and the state of the supply of and demand for labour, together with inflation expectations. As a prelude to examining that relationship let us briefly consider the basic methods employed in the large and still growing literature which has attempted to isolate the separate effects of controls on the pace of wage inflation.[7]

Inflation — with and without controls

The basic method adopted in all the studies which we shall consider is the same and can be described very simply. First, the periods in which controls were not in operation are studied and a quantitative model is developed which explains how wages (and prices) are affected by the state of demand pressure, the state of inflation expectations and other (if any) relevant variables. The model is then used to predict the rate of wage and price change during a period in which controls are in operation. Any systematic differences between the actual behaviour and predicted behaviour of wages and prices is then attributed to the effects of controls. This procedure is not, of course, as reliable as a laboratory experiment in which everything is held constant except for the presence or absence of a controls program and the experiment then repeated a large number of times. It is, however, the nearest we can get to a laboratory experiment in a social science and, provided the statistical work is handled carefully, provides us with the most reliable information available.

The starting point for such studies has been a familiar and intuitively appealing model which describes inflation in the absence of controls and has two propositions. The first proposition is that wage change depends on the excess demand for labour, the expected rate of inflation (usually measured by a weighted average of recent actual rates of inflation) and such factors as the change in the fraction of the labour force unionized. The second proposition is that prices are a markup over unit costs, which in turn are determined by wages, output per head and import prices. Models based on these propositions explain the bulk of the variability of wages and prices in postwar Britain.[8] Such models also fit the Canadian experience very closely.[9]

Predicting the effect of controls

When such models are used to predict the rate of wage and price change during a period of wage-price controls they show that, on the average, with the exception of the Cripps episode, there is no significant downward adjustment of inflation attributable to the controls. The controls do, however, have a temporary effect but one which, in the subsequent development of inflation, is offset and negated. Although individual studies differ in their details, their broad findings agree and to illustrate the calculated effects of controls, we will look at the findings of a study done by Lipsey and Parkin.[10] Chart 4 summarizes their findings.

Chart 4 — Wage Inflation in the United Kingdom 1948-1968

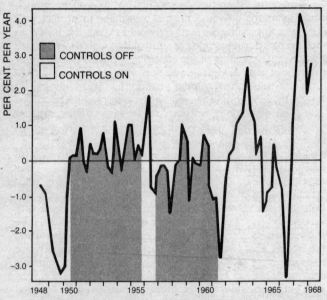

PREDICTION ERRORS OF EQUATION FITTED TO "CONTROLS OFF" PERIODS AND PREDICTION ERRORS OF THAT EQUATION FOR "CONTROLS ON" PERIODS.

Source: Reproduced from Lipsey and Parkin, *op. cit.*, Figure 4.

The chart shows the difference between the actual rate of wage inflation and the rate of wage inflation predicted by the model that Lipsey and Parkin constructed. Because the model is only an approximation to reality there will always be a lack of precision in predicting the rate of wage increase at particular times. However, if the basic determinants of wage inflation stay the same then we should expect the precision of the model to stay the same through time. The shaded areas show the precision of the model during periods when controls were not in effect. As can be seen, the model was usually successful in predicting the percentage change in wages to within one per cent of the actual change.

During periods of wage controls the normal wage-determining process is suspended to the extent that the controls are successful. Therefore, we would not expect the model, which contains only the normal variables, to predict well during such periods. In fact, we would expect the model to make errors during periods of control that would vary in size with the effectiveness of the controls. A positive error larger than about one per cent during the 'controls on' period indicates that the control period produced a larger increase in wages than would otherwise have occurred. A negative value less than about one per cent (negative) indicates that the controls were successful in reducing the rate of wage increase.

Using this criterion let us analyze the various control periods. The first control episode — that of Cripps — was clearly successful. The annual reduction in the rate of wage inflation was almost *two percentage* points. The 1956 episode averaged out at virtually zero. The 1961 freeze was highly successful but for a single quarter only and was followed by some catch-up effects which at least offset the gains during the freeze. This is seen in the chart as the sequence of wage rises in excess of those predicted in the absence of controls peaking at almost 3 per cent in 1963. The 1966 freeze is seen as highly successful but again very short-lived. It lowered wage change by more than three percentage points below the level predicted in the absence of controls. However, it was quickly followed by oversized wage rises of more than four percentage points in 1967.

Controls don't work on wages

The general picture concerning the effects of controls on wages, given the actual degree of labour market demand pressure and state of inflation expectations, is of a successful immediate postwar policy episode followed by a zero average thereafter. The study by Lipsey and Parkin and the large literature which grew out of this work did not explore the effects of the most recent controls introduced at the end of 1972. The only study done recently enough to examine that episode is by Frank J. Reid of the University of Toronto though his study is not yet published.[11] Reid's study whilst more sophisticated than the earlier ones agrees with earlier findings on the success of the Cripps policy and on the temporary success of freezes. He finds that the freeze imposed during the first quarter of 1973 was also successful. However, his conclusions about the overall effectiveness of controls do not differ from my own.

About prices and expectations

The analysis of the effects of controls on the behaviour of wages which we have just reviewed leaves several questions in the air, two of which we now address. The first is, even if controls can temporarily hold wages back, do those effects feed through to prices? Second, do controls affect expectations of inflation, thereby reducing wage and price rises in a way that would be missed by the procedures described above? We take up each of these questions in turn.

The linkage between wages and prices is by no means an exact one even in the absence of controls. We can, however, use the same procedure as described above to calculate that relationship (including an allowance for changes in import prices and productivity) for periods when controls are not operating and then use that relationship to predict the rate of price change which would have taken place given the rates of wage, import price, and productivity change. After conducting such an exercise, Lipsey and Parkin calculated that during the Cripps policy period, prices *rose faster* by three-quarters of a percentage point per annum on the average than predicted, thereby partly though not wholly negating the successful reduction in the rate of wage inflation during that period.[12]

Prices not affected

A similar situation arose during the wage freeze of 1961. The only solidly successful reduction of the rate of price inflation relative to wage inflation was in 1956. For the remainder of the time, there is no discernible change in price behaviour. The implication of this is that, to some extent, 'successful' reductions in the rate of wage change are offset by rising profit margins but, on the whole, the behaviour of prices under a controls program is not very different than would have occurred in the absence of controls.

Expectations

Do controls affect expectations of inflation thereby reducing both wage and price rises in an almost direct manner? This question has been addressed in a study by Carlson and Parkin.[13] Using the results of a monthly survey of individual expectations of future price increases they estimated a time series which measures variations in inflation expectations. The authors determined that inflation expectations are adjusted in the light of current inflation experience but are not influenced by the presence or absence of controls. This is broadly in line with results obtained by a rather different procedure for U.S. experience. For that country, changes in rates of interest on assets with various terms to maturity have been used to make inferences about the relationship between expectations about inflation and the length of time into the future about which expectations are held. Thus, for example, a person investing money for three months is thought to be concerned about (and have expectations about) the inflation rate three months in the future. Similarly for people investing for six months, two years, ten years and so on.

What emerges from these studies is that the short-term (three months ahead) expected inflation rate falls during a freeze but that longer-term expectations are little affected. These results are of course entirely in line with the notion that people form their expectations about economic phenomena in a rational manner using whatever information is available for the purpose. Controls have been seen to fail so often in the past in the U.K. that rational people's expectations are influenced little by their imposition.

IV. SUMMARY OF EFFECTS — IMPLICATIONS FOR CANADA

We have now reviewed (though not reported in detail) the evidence on the effects of wage-price controls on the rate of inflation in the U.K. The central propositions which emerge from that are clear and simple. First, short-term freezes of wages, whether backed by the force of law or not, do lower the rate of wage inflation for the duration of the freeze. Second, prices do not respond as much as wages. Third, after the freeze, there is a catch up in wages which at least offsets the previous gain. The only exception to this pattern is the first postwar restraint period which had more prolonged effects on the rate of wage and price change but, even this period saw greater restraint on wages than on prices. Also, it must be emphasized again, this was a period in which various quantitative controls, such as points rationing schemes and other wartime regulations, were the primary means of allocating resources.

The question still remains however; what does all this imply for Canada? First, it should be remarked that although only U.K. experience has been reviewed above, similar, though less well-documented conclusions seem to emerge for other countries.[14] Also, *the U.S. experience*, which has been very intensively studied, yields conclusions spanned by the two extreme views that *at worst controls had no effect on inflation or at best reduced its rate by a very small and economically and politically unimportant amount.*[15]

In the light of this, if it is to be claimed that what applies to all other countries does not apply to Canada, it is necessary to find special features about this country which make it unique in this particular respect. To a recent refugee from Britain, Canada's economy appears to have much in common with that of Britain. Of course, Canada is much richer but, in terms of labour relations, monetary policy, fiscal policy and state intervention the two economies are very similar. Also, in terms of interdependence with other countries, there are similarities. None of these guarantee that Canada's inflation will be as unresponsive to controls as Britain's was but they all point in that direction.

V. THE SIDE EFFECTS OF CONTROLS IN THE U.K.

Four major side effects of controls were identified in the introduction to this chapter: resource misallocation, income redistribution, a deterioration in industrial relations, and an increasing disregard for the rule of law. We now examine those assertions more fully. Unfortunately, important though these areas are, they are less-easily documented and have been less-comprehensively studied than the effects of controls on the rate of inflation itself. However, there is a good deal that can be said.

On misuse of resources

First let us look at resource misallocations. The most clear and obvious resource reallocation that takes place when comprehensive wage-price controls are introduced is that involved with the very process of administration of the controls. First, a statutory agency of some kind is usually set up which typically takes the cream of the civil service and brings in talented people from industry and the labour unions as well as from the legal and accounting professions. This, however, is just the tip of the iceberg. Just as government has to set up its own statutory body to handle the controls so major unions and firms have to hire specialist services to plead with, argue with, and make cases to the statutory body. It is very hard to quantify the loss from this resource reallocation and it indeed has been variable. Some controls in the British case hardly used any resources of this type at all but others, most notably that set up in the middle 1960's under the National Board for Prices and Incomes, absorbed an enormous amount of scarce talent.

The classical economic analysis of resource misallocation, in the face of relative prices that do not reflect market conditions, probably does not apply very seriously to the operation of wage-price controls. If the controls were totally inflexible and made rigidly to stick then such misallocations would occur and possibly indeed they do occur on a relatively limited scale for those short periods (usually not longer than three months) when controls have been absolutely rigid. However, I suspect that the resources expended in evading the controls are sufficient to ensure that relative prices do adjust to reflect underlying changes in supply and demand. Precisely how this is achieved will depend on the nature of the control regime.

Often it is possible to avoid the controls while remaining within the letter of the law. On the prices front this is most easily done by the skilful use of inventory and asset valuations designed to produce a particular impression concerning movements in unit costs. On the wages front there are sufficient possibilities for regrading workers so that, although the pay scales for particular jobs stay within the guidelines, the actual wages earned by any particular individual goes outside those limits. On occasions, however, it has been easier to avoid the controls by actions which are technically illegal. In these cases it is terribly hard, indeed impossible in the absence of court cases of which there have been very few, to provide documentary evidence. However, it was common knowledge (but based entirely on hearsay) that many British firms during the most recent phase of wage-price controls were evading the controls by writing invoices which sold output to subsidiaries overseas and then reimporting the material from the overseas subsidiary or agent at a price sufficiently high to ensure that their costs as a result of rising import costs were adequately large to justify the price which they wanted to charge for their output. In order to do this it was not necessary to incur the shipping costs of actually exporting and reimporting the goods. All that was necessary was to generate the documentation. This, of course, is a very simple procedure to pursue and almost an impossible one to police.

Although I have suggested that the classical resource misallocations arising from the fixing of disequilibrium relative prices are probably not serious in most cases, there is one aspect of the way in which controls were applied in Britain which appears at least in part to be a feature of the Canadian controls — a feature which probably did have an adverse effect on resource allocation. That is the tendency for wage controls to be written in such a way that they discriminate against the more highly-paid members of the community. In Britain there were often limits specified in terms of the flat rate of money increase. This of course would translate into a much smaller percentage increase for the better off than the poorest members of the community. Canada has a similar clause in its wage control program in that it imposes a $2,400 limit increase. This means that all people making more than $24,000 per annum will be limited to a percentage rise which is less than the average. Of course, it is usually sought to justify this type of arrangement in terms of equity arguments. However, that misses the point. High wages are paid to those whose output is most valuable. If a government regulation tells employers that they may not pay their highly-skilled workers as much as they are worth, then firms will either have to find other ways of compensating those employees or run the risk of losing some of their services.

At the other extreme in the British case, although this does not appear at the present time to be a feature of the current Canadian policy, lower paid workers were more favoured than average workers. The permissible wage rise of the lower paid has been higher than the average, and has become the minimum as well as the maximum raise possible. This, of course, is exactly like a minimum wage law. It has the effect of pricing out of the labour market certain lower skilled and low marginal product workers. It therefore raises the unemployment rate amongst those classes of workers and carries with it the risk that the government will misread the resulting rise in unemployment and see it as a signal to stimulate aggregate demand, thereby generating even more inflationary pressures for the controls to attempt to contain.

A more serious consequence of the policy is the way in which price controls have been applied in the public sector especially during the recent 'social contract'. Government subsidies have been widely used in an attempt to hold down the price of public sector produced gas, electricity, public housing and public transport. Also, food has been subsidized. This has resulted in an enormous increase in the public sector deficit and borrowing requirement and far from reducing inflationary pressures has exacerbated them. This may be particularly relevant for Canada where oil is still being sold at too low a price relative to the world price.

On the redistribution of income

The second major area in which controls have side effects is in the arbitrary redistribution of income which they cause. The first feature worth looking at here is that between labour income on the one hand and profits on the other.

Chart 5 — Income from Employment as a Percentage of Gross Domestic Product, United Kingdom 1952-1974

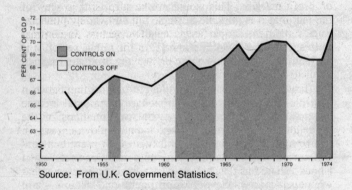

Source: From U.K. Government Statistics.

Chart 5 illustrates the share of employment income in the post-war years. Here we see that income from employment as a percentage of gross domestic product fell between 1952 and 1953, then climbed to 1956, fell slightly down to 1959, then rose to a peak in '62 when it fell for one year, then rose to another peak in 1966 when it fell for one year, then, after peaking in 1968-69 took a prolonged slide down to 1973 after which it surged forward again. Taking the period as a whole there has been a tendency for the share of income from employment in national income to rise. That share in 1952 was a little over 66 per cent and by 1974 had reached almost 72 per cent.

The factors making for that trend increase in the share of employment income would take us beyond the scope of this study. Furthermore, there is still a good deal of controversy surrounding that question. It seems likely that at least one of the main contributing factors has been the increased market power of labour that arises from a persistent commitment to a full employment program. However, despite the fact that there has been a trend increase in income from employment, there have been five occasions on which labour's share has fallen. Four of those are associated with the application of wage-price controls. This suggests that controls bite more heavily on employment income than they do on prices of final output and than they do, therefore, on profit margins. This would not be surprising in view of the fact that it is possible to single out and widely publicize wage settlements in particular sensitive sectors. In contrast to this, outside a few key products in the public sector, it is very difficult to pin down one or two key products for high publicity and rigid control.

It would be foolish to claim that the connection between controls and the dips in labour's share in national income are at all strong. There are several continuations of the reduction in the share of income from employment which run beyond a control period and two which precede a control period. Thus there are periods outside controls when labour's share has fallen. However, what is noticeable is that whenever controls have been in operation, labour's share has also fallen. This is not to say that because controls apparently have some potential for curbing the rise in labour's share that they are therefore doing a good job. There are other ways in which labour's share could be controlled if indeed it was desirable to control it; most notably by generating a competitive environment in labour markets which made workers responsible for getting their supply price right rather than placing all the responsibility for employment on the aggregate demand management policies of the government.

Much less easy to document are movements of relative wages which result from controls. There must be a strong presumption that the weak will lose under a control regime despite clauses favouring low wage groups. Governments usually try to avoid head-on confrontations with major and powerful groups of organized labour and therefore one way or another wage settlements for such groups are likely to be further from the guidelines and closer to the original claims than are those of weaker groups.

Also, not at all well-documented but highly likely, are redistributions within the corporate sector arising from the fact that some prices are more easily pegged than others. Highly-standardized products, for example, are easier to police than are highly-specialized items.

Possibly the most serious arbitrary redistribution of income in the British control experiments has been within the public sector and between the public and private sectors. Within the public sector there has been a great deal of wage disparity. As a rough approximation it seems reasonable to say that the private sector has probably on the average not been much affected by controls. In the public sector the administrators and those directly and indirectly involved in the administration of the state's increasing economic interventionism have done very well. Real wages of administrative civil servants in Britain have increased as rapidly as those of any group in the economy. However, other public sector employees such as doctors, nurses, refuse collectors, teachers, academics and the like have all lost out over the past few years. Thus, the general pattern is that the administrative civil servants have done best, private sector employees have about held their own, while other public sector workers lost.

On industrial relations and strikes

The third major area in which controls have had a clear and devastating effect on the British economy has been in industrial relations. The British strike record is one of the most widely-known facts about that country in the rest of the world. That strike record, in terms of number of working days lost each year, is set out in Chart 6. What is significant about that chart is the strong trend growth in working days lost all through the 1960's. The very high peak of almost 24 million working days lost in 1972 is due almost entirely to the introduction in 1971 of the 'infamous' Industrial Relations Act. That Act, introduced by a Conservative government, generated a great deal of hostility from the labour

Chart 6 — Strikes in the United Kingdom, Number of Working Days Lost Annually 1947-1974

Source: U.K. Department of Employment Gazette.

movement and industrial relations in the period were very bad for reasons completely unconnected with controls. However, apart from that peak it is clear that controls have been associated with a tendency for the frequency of strikes to rise. The only exception to this is the relatively placid period of the immediate postwar years, at a time when there was a certain euphoric support for the first postwar Labour Government on the part of the newly-demobilized labour force.

In the period of the middle 1950's and throughout the 1960's we see that the more controls were prolonged, the higher was the volume of strike activity. This also seems to have applied during the reintroduction of controls in 1973-74. Of course, correlation does not prove causation. There seem to be three possibilities: i) controls cause strikes, ii) strikes cause inflation which lead to controls, and iii) some third outside factor both generates controls and strikes. The obvious candidate in this latter case is inflation itself. That is, a rising inflation rate could be thought of as both bringing on controls and generating more strikes. Unscrambling these three alternative possible causation theories is not at all straightforward. However, if we try to explain the variability of the inflation rate using the conventional hypothesis that the rate of inflation is higher the higher is the state of inflation expectations and the greater is the pressure on aggregate demand then we find that we can explain pretty well all of the variability of Britain's inflation rate and that there is no independent role left for strikes.[16] Thus, it seems fairly safe to conclude that strikes do not cause inflation.

Does inflation cause strikes though? In a study of the determination of strike activity in the British economy, Pencavel[17] has shown that there is a partial correlation between inflation and strikes. However, we must be very cautious how we interpret this correlation. *A priori* there seems no reason at all why a high rate of inflation should lead to high volume of strike activity. We would expect strikes to arise because of a mismatching of expectations about inflation between the two sides of industry. On the face of it, it is very difficult to see why the two sides of industry should take different views about the rate of inflation in a way that is systematically related to the degree of inflation. It seems much more likely that both sides of industry take broadly the same view but that because of government regulation labour unions need to demonstrate more strongly their determination to see their expectations given effect to.

Although one cannot be sure, it seems that the most plausible interpretation of the persistent increase in strike activity in the 1960's and the upturn again in 1973-74 is that it was caused by the government placing itself in a situation of confrontation with labour unions leaving them with the option of accepting a cut in real wages or using their market power, displayed through the strike weapon; faced with these alternatives, organized labour has opted for the latter.

On respect for the rule of law

This leads naturally into the final major and perhaps most dangerous side-effect of controls, namely the disrespect which they engender for the rule of law. The most effective way of ridiculing a legal system is to enact laws which have no way of being implemented. Perhaps the best example is that of King Canute standing on the beach and ordering the tide to stop. Although it looks less ridiculous it is in the same category of laws for a parliament to legislate that wages and prices will not rise or will not rise by more than a certain amount. It is akin to attempting by statute to repeal the law of gravity. When, as would be predicted, the law begins to be ignored or worse, when strong and well-organized groups line up against the law, this raises questions concerning the sovereignty and authority of parliament. In Britain, especially during the most recent phase of controls in 1974, this reached the amazing pitch of leading to a general election campaign on the central theme "Who Governs Britain - Whitehall or the Unions?" That particular episode illustrates this point most vividly.

In the winter of 1973-1974 following the oil price rise of the fall of 1973 a major pay claim was put in to the Heath Government by the coal miners in the U.K. The miners had by that time suffered a relative fall in wages largely as a result of their weakening competitive position in a world of cheap alternative sources of fuel and of a declining industry. However, as a result of the oil price rise, coal became a more viable source of energy. Also, the miners union was somewhat more centrally and tightly organized by 1974 than it had been in earlier years. The combination of these two things enabled the coal miners to put in a large but, many would have judged, not unrealistic wage claim. The claim, however, was well outside the guidelines of the prices and incomes control program then in force. The Conservative Government dug in its toes, refused to meet the miners' demands and this led to a prolonged and very costly coal strike. The strike led to a massive reduction in electricity generation and eventually to most of the British economy moving onto a three day working week. This particular episode serves to illustrate, in fact, all four major side-effect arguments that have been advanced above. Here we have a clear case in which the controls led to a massive reduction in economic welfare as a result of lost output. They also were an attempt to force through an arbitrary distribution of income in opposition to undoubted market forces pointing in the direction of an increase in the relative wage of coal miners; they produced a crisis in industrial relations close to the proportions of the British General Strike of 1926 and finally brought about the fall of the Heath Government in February 1974.

Of course, it could be argued that the particular policies being pursued by that particular government at that particular time were very unfortunate and were not of the essence of wage-price controls but just one extreme example of them. True, that episode was extreme, but it is the extremes that most vividly illustrate the dangers in pursuing policies such as these.

It has been argued that controls are counter-productive and that they do not control inflation and in addition have damaging side-effects. It may be thought that Britain's current control program contradicts to some degree these conclusions since with the latest episode of controls in operation, the rate of inflation is reported to be moderating. However, it would be wrong to attribute that inflation moderation to controls. Monetary policy has been on a severely contractionary path since mid-1972 and it is that which has produced the present unemployment level of one million plus and has reduced the inflation rate. The lesson from the latest British experiment with controls is entirely in line with that of the previous episodes.

Notes

[1] The title of the Policy Statement tabled in the House of Commons by Donald S. Macdonald, Minister of Finance, October 14, 1975.

[2] Among the earliest price and wage controls were those of Diocletian in the third century A.D.

[3] Arthur W. Marget, *The Theory of Prices*, Vol. 1, Kelly, New York 1966, Reprint of Economic Classics edition gives a superb and thorough history of the theory of money up to the middle 1930's.

[4]For a detailed survey of the debate on the question, see David Laidler and Michael Parkin, "Inflation: A Survey," *Economic Journal*, December, 1975; Michael Parkin, "The Causes of Inflation: Recent Contributions and Current Controversies," in Parkin and Nobay (Eds) *Current Economic Problems*, Cambridge University Press, 1975; and Michael Parkin, "Where is Britain's Inflation Going?," *Lloyds Bank Review*, July 1975, Number 117, p. 1-13. (Note that there are some discrepancies between the charts in the present chapter and in the Lloyds Bank Review article. Those in this chapter are correct.)

[5]The narrow money supply is used because there are good reasons to believe the broader definitions to contain serious distortions, especially in 1971-3. (See my Lloyds Bank Review article referred to in footnote (4) above.)

[6]The 1964 starting date is selected because Britain's money supply data were not compiled on a comparable basis prior to that year.

[7]For a convenient though somewhat technical summary source of much of that literature, see *Incomes Policy and Inflation* edited by Michael Parkin and Michael T. Sumner, University of Toronto Press, 1974.

[8]For a detailed survey see Parkin, "The Causes of Inflation," *op. cit.*

[9]To fit the facts of the late 1960's and 70's in both Britain and Canada, it is necessary to allow for the fact that the meaning of unemployment has changed as an indicator of labour market demand pressure due to considerable improvements in unemployment compensation rates relative to net wages.

[10]See Richard G. Lipsey and Michael Parkin, "Incomes Policy: A Reappraisal," *Economica*, May 1970, reprinted as Chapter 4 in Parkin and Sumner (Eds), *Incomes Policy and Inflation*, University of Toronto Press, 1974. See also for a survey of the econometric evidence on the effects of incomes policy-wage price controls, Chapter 1 of that volume.

[11]Frank J. Reid, "The Rotation Hypothesis of Incomes Policy: An Empirical Test for the U.K., 1948-1973," University of Toronto, Department of Political Economy, 100 St. George Street, Toronto 5. (Mimeo)

[12]See Lipsey and Parkin, *op. cit.*, Figure 5 and discussion.

[13]John A. Carlson and Michael Parkin, "Inflation Expectations," *Economica*, May 1975.

[14]See especially Lloyd Ullman and Robert J. Flanagan, *Wage Restraints: A Study of Incomes Policies in Western Europe*, University of California Press, 1971.

[15]On the United States see Michael Parkin, "The 1973 Report of the President's Council of Economic Advisers: A Critique," *American Economic Review*, Vol. LXIII, No. 4, September, 1973 and the other works referred to in the bibliography of that article.

[16]See Laidler and Parkin, *op. cit.*

[17]See John H. Pencavel, "An Investigation into Industrial Strike Activity in Britain," *Economica*, N.S., vol. 37 (147) p. 239-56.

The Post-War Record

The U.S. Economic Stabilization Program of 1971-1974

MICHAEL R. DARBY

Associate Professor of Economics
University of California at Los Angeles

THE AUTHOR

Michael R. Darby was born in Dallas, Texas in 1945 and was graduated from Dartmouth College in 1967 before taking his PhD. at the University of Chicago in 1971. Professor Darby taught at Ohio State University as an Assistant Professor before moving to the University of California at Los Angeles where he is presently Associate Professor of Economics. During 1975 Professor Darby was on academic leave as Harry Scherman Research Fellow, National Bureau of Economic Research, New York.

Professor Darby's recent publications include a text book, *Macroeconomics: The Theory of Income, Employment and the Price Level*, McGraw Hill, New York, 1976. Other scholarly works of Professor Darby recently appeared in the *Quarterly Journal of Economics*, ("The Permanent Income Theory of Consumption: A Restatement", May, 1974) and the *Journal of Political Economy*, ("Three-and-a-Half Million U.S. Employees Have Been Mislaid: or, an Explanation of Unemployment, 1934-1941", February, 1976).

The Post-War Record

The U.S. Economic Stabilization Program of 1971-1974*

MICHAEL R. DARBY

Associate Professor of Economics
University of California at Los Angeles

I. INTRODUCTION

President Richard M. Nixon announced his Economic Stabilization Program (ESP) on August 15, 1971. This program — popularly termed price and wage controls — was initially immensely popular and similar programs were soon established in other countries. The program expired on April 30, 1974, after an election-year Congress refused to renew authorization. This paper examines the nature and effects of the program as it evolved over time.

The most surprising feature of the program was that nearly the only enforced restrictive ceiling was that on increases in wages in unionized firms. In effect, the ESP was little more than a scheme for regulating the monopoly power of unions. When this rein was relaxed in January 1973, the program became a shell imposing administrative costs on many industries and serious effects in a few, but mostly 'full of sound and fury, signifying nothing'.

*This study summarizes, integrates, and extends the author's earlier technical studies "Price and Wage Controls: The First Two Years" and "Price and Wage Controls: Further Evidence" in K. Brunner and A. Meltzer (eds.), *Carnegie-Rochester Conference Series*, Vol. II, Amsterdam: North-Holland, in press.

The ESP is generally credited with reducing the rate of inflation during the first eighteen months of its existence, but in the last fifteen months inflation was recorded at a higher rate than would otherwise have occurred as prices 'caught up'. Taken as a whole, the ESP did not appear to have any effect on the average rate of inflation from the second quarter of 1971 to the third quarter of 1974. The reported swings in the rate of inflation appear to reflect initial hidden reductions in the quality of products. Such reductions were undertaken to avoid administrative costs involved in making large explicit price changes. After January 1973, these administrative costs were reduced or eliminated and firms began to restore quality.

II. ORIGINS OF THE AMERICAN INFLATION

Price and wage controls were politically popular in the United States in 1971 because of widespread dissatisfaction with the rate of inflation then being experienced. Controls were popularly interpreted as strong political action to 'do something' about inflation.

The causes of inflation

Persistent inflation is always and everywhere a monetary phenomenon, as has been ably demonstrated by other essays in this series. That is, leaving aside year-to-year wiggles around the basic trend, the price level grows if, and to the extent that, money is created faster than the normal growth in the public's desire for money expressed in terms of the real goods and services that it can buy. The average price of goods and services must rise because until it does people will think that they have more cash than they desire and attempt to adjust their position by spending the 'excess'. This process will continue until prices rise and people's desire for cash correspondingly rises to absorb the available supply.

This relation is not perfect over any short period of time. In particular, prices and wages do not adjust immediately to an increased rate of money creation and so later must rise faster for a time — like a late starter in a race — to catch up. This cyclical adjustment of the rate of inflation to a change in the growth rate of the money supply is the source of much confusion. At first, an increased rate of money creation induces increased spending and little increase in inflation so that real spending grows abnormally rapidly and unemployment falls. In time, workers increase their wage demands and inflation and unemployment rise while growth of real income and spending becomes abnormally slow. The growth rates of wages and prices seem disproportionate to the growth of money during this catch-up period and talk of 'cost-push inflation' becomes popular. When the catch-up is completed, the rate of inflation falls but to a rate higher than existed before the increase in the rate of money creation.[1]

Pre-control monetary policy in the U.S.

As in all industrialized countries, the growth rate of the U.S. money supply is determined by the central bank — in the case of the U.S., the Federal Reserve System, popularly called the Fed. For complex reasons peripheral to this paper, the Fed's monetary policy from 1963 to the start of controls can be characterized as accelerating money creation, except for slow-downs in the second half of 1966 and in 1969. As a direct result, the trend rate of inflation also accelerated, to the protest of the populace and the discomfort of the politicians.

The wage-price spiral

Politicians of course denied blame for the results of government policy and instead encouraged myths attributing inflation to greedy businessmen and greedy unionists. Increased inflation implies more rapid growth in prices and wages, but these are symptoms not causes. Still, businessmen were quite willing to hang any charge on unionists and so popularized the myth with respect to their adversaries. Unionists were pleased to return the compliment. With so much propaganda laying blame for inflation to the monopoly power of business or unionists, the public and press largely overlooked the undramatic money supply data and the careful complaints of academics. So the pressure rose to do something about the supposed villains.

III. THE NATURE AND EFFECTS OF THE ECONOMIC STABILIZATION PROGRAM

On August 15, 1971, President Nixon announced the imposition of a 90-day freeze on all prices, rents, wages and salaries except for raw agricultural products and imports. This action, variously termed as Freeze I or Phase I, was taken under authority of the Economic Stabilization Act of 1970, as amended. The Act had been passed by a Democratic Congress in an election year to provide debating ammunition against the Republican President who had pledged not to use the 'standby' authority to control prices and wages.

Phase I (Freeze I) was followed by Phase II, Phase III, Freeze II, and Phase IV, each with significantly different rules and regulations. The essential features and effects of each phase will be considered separately below.

Leaving aside the brief freezes, the basic philosophy of the controls was a cost-plus theory of pricing. A typical statement was:

> "The standards announced by the Pay Board and the Price Commission imply the following arithmetic: If compensation per hour of work rises by 5.5 per cent per annum, and if output per hour of work rises by 3 per cent per annum, labor costs per unit of output will rise by approximately 2.5 per cent per annum. If prices rise in the same proportion as labor costs, which are the largest element in total costs for the economy as a whole, then prices will also rise by 2.5 per cent, a rate within the range of the goal set by the CLC."[2]

Price and wage rules were set relative to historical base periods for individual firms and there was no uniformity in permissable prices or wages between firms.

Exemptions were granted based on the size of firms (for prices), on the number of employees (for wages), on the industry, and on the level of wages.[3]

Phase I

The initial Freeze was a surprise action aimed at avoiding strategic price and wage increases while a more sophisticated control program was formulated and implemented.

Just prior to the Freeze, the rate of inflation was running about 4.5 per cent per annum; so after the end of a 90-day freeze the level of prices would be about one percentage point below the level that market forces would have produced if the market price level had continued to grow at about the same rate as previously. Even this is a high estimate of the difference between what we might call the 'ceiling' and the 'market' price levels however. Since the growth rate of wages normally exceeds the growth rate of prices by the amount of productivity growth, a successful freeze on wages might cause the price level to fall over time. If this is to happen, the freeze on wages must not result in labor shortages. In fact, firms were able to hire increased quantities of labor at the frozen wage scales and employment grew at the rapid rate of 4.2 per cent per annum from August to November, 1971.

Wages the target

The major economic rationalization for the ESP was that the wage demands of nonunionized workers[4] and the agreed wages in union contracts included a substantial adjustment for expected inflation. It was argued that the ESP could speed the adjustment to a lower rate of inflation by reducing inflationary expectations and abrogating union contracts. Thus the temporary increase in unemployment that would have been associated with a decrease in the growth rate of the money supply would be reduced or eliminated. As will be shown below, the Fed increased money supply growth to new heights during the Freeze instead of reducing it. Nevertheless, during the brief life of the Freeze the hoped-for reduction (or perhaps postponement) of wage increases seems to have occurred.

The price feeeze restricted most prices only trivially if at all; the market price for some goods actually rose significantly because of increased demand or cost conditions. This was especially true for restaurant meals and processed foods as prices of raw agricultural products were exempt from controls. Where it was difficult to conceal reductions in quality or portions, products became unavailable except in new higher priced 'deluxe' versions (the cherry-on-the-top phenomenon).

Phase II - Wage and price controls?

The Phase II program (November 14, 1971 - January 10, 1973) bore little resemblance to standard ideas of price and wage controls. No economy-wide regulations were issued as to maximum permissable prices for certain products or maximum permissable wage rates for certain types of labor. Instead regulations were applied on a firm-by-firm basis. Subject to exceptions and exemptions, there were three key constraints imposed on firms: (1) Profit margins were limited to the average of the best two of the three fiscal years preceeding Phase I. (2) Wage scales were limited to a 5.5 per cent per annum rate of growth. (3) Large firms had to obtain prior approval for any increase in prices (firms with sales of $100 million or more) or wages (firms with 5000 employees or more). These constraints, as well as other subsidiary regulations, were supposed to be enforced by a staff of less than 4000 people.[5]

The price formula

The general standard for price increases was that prices could increase proportionately to increases in costs. But this is exactly what happens in any pure inflation and so provided no real constraint for most firms. Only where major shifts in relative demand or supply increased the market return to factors of production owned by the firm — notably in the lumber, oil, and leather industries — was the profit margin rule a serious limit. Most firms required only a little creative accounting[6] to meet the profit margin ceiling.

With prices essentially uncontrolled — so long as they rose in normal proportion to costs — the program could affect the rate of inflation only by reducing the rate at which costs were growing. This was the role of the wage controls.

Wage controls

Generally wage controls are very easy to evade as long as employer and employee both find it advantageous to do so. For example, the number of hours worked can be over-reported or a spurious promotion made with no real change in duties. It will be in the interest of employers in competitive labor markets to evade the controls as otherwise they will lose employees to those who do so.

Unions the target

This is not true for unionized firms. U.S. labor laws in effect give unions the power to impose considerably higher wages than required to obtain the number of employees that the firm is willing to hire at those wages. Under the ESP, the maximum wage demands that firms would be required by the courts to meet were limited to a 5.5 per cent per annum increase. Nearly all unionized firms could still hire all the employees they desired under the controlled wage rate and so had no incentive to evade the wage controls. In effect, the government imposed a price regulation on the unions who had previously been granted monopoly power. It may not be surprising that the Nixon administration should use the Economic Stabilization Act to benefit the owners of unionized firms at the expense of union leaders and members[7] given the general support of the former and opposition of the latter in the 1968 and 1972 Presidential elections.

Generally, firms in competitive markets could and did easily evade the wage ceiling where it was less than the market wage. Unionized firms were quite willing to abide by the reduced wage scales. The only real enforcement of the wage ceiling was the unwillingness of the courts and the ESP administration to approve union contracts which exceeded it by much. Little actual evasion was required by nonunionized firms as low-wage and small-firm exemptions excluded most private nonfarm workers from any controls.[8] Significantly, the small-firm exemption did not apply to the heavily-unionized construction industry regulated under the Pay Board's Construction Industry Stabilization Committee.

Effects on wages and employment

The impact of the controls on union wages was to increase the number of workers which unionized firms were willing to hire. As a result some workers were shifted from less productive work in non-unionized forms to more productive work in unionized firms and total output increased. Unfortunately, there is no satisfactory way to estimate the precise net increase in total output which resulted. Earlier estimates of the reduction in U.S. real output due to unions' monopoly power to set wage rates were approximately 0.3 per cent of gross national product at most.[9] So although the precise increase in output due to the reduction in union power is unknown, it must have been at most about one quarter of one per cent. Even if the demand for money in terms of real goods and services were increased proportionately,[10] this would imply at most a 0.25 per cent decrease in the price level compared to what it would otherwise have been. So the increase in real output and the reduction in the price level due to Phase II wage controls were both relatively trivial.

Prices up, quality down

About 1700 large firms were required to obtain prior approval from the Price Commission in order to raise prices. In granting increases, the Price Commission did not adhere to the general regulations. For example, the excess of wage increases over 5.5 per cent per annum even where approved by the Pay Board due to some provision of law might not be included in allowable costs. Historical averages of industry productivity growth were substituted for firm-by-firm experience. However 'cost justified' large price increases were not approved. Firms could and did avoid the administrative costs of separate applications by entering into 'term limit pricing' agreements permitting them to raise prices at an average rate of, say, 1.8 to 2.0 per cent per annum with no single price to be increased by more than an agreed amount such as 8 per cent.

Although stated prices were controlled, there was no staff on the Price Commission to attempt to control the quality of goods. So firms which would otherwise have increased prices by 4 per cent were free to increase prices by the approved amount, say 2.5 per cent, and to make up the difference by reducing quality so that unit costs fell, in this case by 1.5 per cent. So long as the quality reduction was covert and profit margins did not exceed the firm's allowable limit, no penalties were incurred.

Government statistical agencies find it difficult to correct for quality changes in normal times; it is therefore not surprising that they should miss most such covert deterioration in quality. As a result, the reported price index appears to have fallen steadily below the 'true' price level — the price level adjusted for the changing quality of goods — during Phase II. Section III below presents estimates of the true changes in the price level adjusted for such omitted changes in quality. These estimates indicate that the reported price index rose about 0.2 per cent per month or 2.5 per cent per annum less than the true price level.

Phase II controls were generally quite popular except with unionists. The President had taken apparently dramatic and effective action which reduced the apparent rate of inflation with virtually no allocative ill effects.[11] Nevertheless, with the Presidential election over in November 1972 and increasing popular doubt about the reported low rates of inflation, the program had outlived its political usefulness by the end of the year and change was in order.

Phase III

The Phase III program (January 11, 1973 through June 12, 1973) removed the requirements for prior approval of price increases except in a few listed industries. The profit margin limitation remained in force as did the 5.5 per cent per annum standard for wage increases. Prior approval of wage increases was largely discontinued as well.

The main change was the removal of the requirement that large firms receive prior — and arbitrarily limited — approval of price increases. As a result, these firms were free to increase their prices not only in proportion to the increase in costs required to produce a unit of given quality but also in proportion to the increased costs necessary to restore the previously degraded quality. So whereas in Phase II the rate of inflation had been consistently *underreported* in the official price indices, with the beginning of Phase III the rate of inflation was *overreported* because of a failure to correct for the restoration of quality.

For these reasons, the consumer price index rose at a rate of 9.0 per cent per annum from January to June 1973 as compared to 3.5 per cent per annum from July 1972 to January 1973. In something of a panic Phase III was abandoned.

Freeze II and Phase IV - Opposition becomes unanimous

Freeze II (June 13, 1973 to August 11, 1973) was imposed to permit reformulation of stricter controls. All prices except rents and raw agricultural products at first sale were frozen at their June 1-8 levels. Wages, however, were allowed to rise as under Phase III. So, unlike the first freeze, firms faced price ceilings which fell relative to the market level of prices.

Shortages and outright cheating became more common. Food shortages in grocery stores forced the administration to begin Phase IV food regulations on July 18, 1973.

The fiasco which was Freeze II was soon replaced with Phase IV (August 12, 1973 to April 30, 1974). Phase IV continued the relaxed Phase III wage controls and reinstated Phase II requirements for prior notification and approval of price increases by the largest firms, with the exception that applications not acted on in 30 days could be implemented. This permitted the ESP administration to allow price increases where required to avoid shortages without any explicit approval. The profit margin limit was replaced with a limit on the dollar amount of net income per unit — profits were permitted to increase only in proportion to unit sales.

The unit profit limit was hard to enforce but was sufficiently restrictive that most remaining supporters of controls on the business side joined unionists in opposition. Much of the general public had also lost its naive faith in the efficacy of controls.

Besting the bulge

The main thrust of Phase IV, however, was gradual decontrol. At the end of Phase II, owing to its failure to account for the decline in quality, the government price index underreported the 'true' price level by about 4 per cent. By the end of Phase III, this difference was reduced to about 2.5 per cent.[12] The main objective of Phase IV was to spread the 'bulge' in the reported rate of inflation over as long a period as possible. The idea is a simple one; if the true rate of inflation were a constant 6 per cent per annum and the 2.5 per cent gap between the reported and true price indices were eliminated over a year, then the reported rate of inflation for that year would be 8.5 per cent per annum. If instead the gap was eliminated over six months, the price index would rise in those six months 5.5 per cent or 11 per cent per annum which would look much more alarming.

In the first four months of Phase IV, industries were selected for decontrol primarily to eliminate or prevent shortages of basic materials. As it became increasingly unlikely that an extension of the Economic Stabilization Act would pass Congress, the pace of decontrol accelerated in 1974. The Cost of Living Council (the ESP administrative body) devised a technique for spreading the inflation bulge beyond the expiration of controls. This was to exchange decontrol for an agreement by the major firms in an industry as to pricing policy for some months after control. As the April 30th expiration date became a certainty, the Council's ability to persuade firms to enter such agreements dried up.

IV. PRICES AND OUTPUT UNDER THE ESP

Now that we have set out the main features of the various phases and freezes, we can examine the impact on prices and output of the Economic Stabilization Program as a whole. In doing so, we are necessarily comparing what *did happen* with our best estimate of what *would have happened* in the absence of the ESP. No conclusive answer can, of course, be given as to either what was or what might have been, but reasonably good approximations seem possible. In view of the experimentation now underway in Canada, it seems much more than an academic exercise to engage in such speculation.

Reported inflation rates

Let us first examine what *did* happen. Figure 1 shows the rate of inflation as measured by the 'price deflator for gross national product (GNP deflator)'. This price series is calculated for each quarter by the government as the ratio of two numbers. The number in the top of the ratio is the government's estimate of total spending in the economy during the quarter. The number in the bottom of the ratio is the government's estimate of the value of total spending in terms of prices that prevailed in some base or benchmark period. Calculated in this way, the price series has a value of 1. in the base period and values in subsequent periods that reflect movements in the prices of goods away from their level in the base period. The price series calculated in this way is called a 'deflator' because it can be used to deflate or translate current spending estimates into spending estimates at base year prices. The GNP deflator is the U.S. price series with the broadest coverage and includes price information about the whole range of spending in the U.S. As is evident from Figure 1, the reported growth rate of the GNP deflator during Freeze I and Phase II (third quarter 1971 through

Figure 1 — U.S. Inflation rates as estimated by the GNP Deflator, 1970-1975

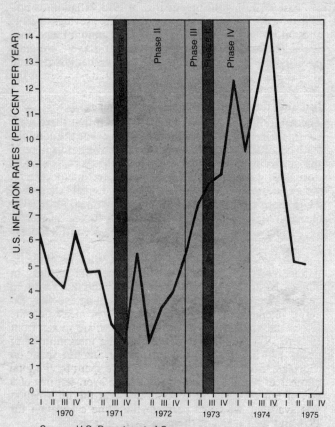

Source: U.S. Department of Commerce.

fourth quarter 1972) dropped to 3.2 per cent per annum compared to an average inflation rate of 5.2 per cent per annum in the preceeding six quarters. Shortly after the advent of Phase III during the first quarter of 1973, inflation, as estimated by the GNP deflator, rose above the previous average and did not return to the 5 per cent per annum range until the second and third quarters of 1975. It is therefore quite easy to understand the popular impression that Phases I and II were effective in reducing the rate of inflation whereas the rest of the ESP was not.

Inflation rates corrected for quality changes

The earlier discussion of Phase II showed that there were considerable incentives for large firms to evade the administrative limits on price increases through covert reductions in the quality of their products. In later phases relaxation of prior approval and decontrol permitted restoration of previously degraded quality. The nature of the ESP thus leads us to suspect that price increases (corrected for quality changes) were *underreported* through the fourth quarter of 1972 and thereafter overreported until the decontrol process was complete.

Fortunately, there is a way to obtain estimates of the inflation rate (the GNP deflator) corrected for changes in quality. Before considering how I actually did that I want to give an example of how it is done using a more everyday example. Suppose that we were interested in measuring the rate of increase in the price of hot chocolate mixes from 1973 to 1974. Suppose that we knew the total number of boxes sold in 1973 and the total dollar amount spent on chocolate mixes; by dividing total dollars spent by the total number of boxes sold we would get the average price of a box of hot chocolate mix. Assuming that the information was available, we could perform the same calculation for 1974 and then calculate the percentage increase.

The situation would be made more complicated if we had reason to believe that the quality of the mix had changed from one year to the next. Suppose, for example, we found that 1.5 teaspoons of the 1974 vintage were required to brew an excellent cup whereas only 1 teaspoon of the 1973 mix was required — a difference caused by the percentage of cocoa in the mix. We would have to conclude that

147

the quality of the mix had fallen. As a result, our price calculation would have to be adjusted to reflect the decline in quality. One method of making the adjustment that parallels the method of adjustment that I use later to correct the GNP deflator can be described as follows.

The nature of the ordinary calculation described above is essentially that of dividing a total spending number (dollars spent on chocolate mixes) by a measure of quantity or output (number of boxes of mix sold). By simply using a different, quality-adjusted measure of output with the same total spending number we arrive at a quality-adjusted price of chocolate mix in 1973 and 1974. In the present case, it would be appropriate to use the number of ounces of raw cocoa used in the preparation of one box as an adjustment factor to derive an adjusted output number. Having done this we would find that hot chocolate mix had increased in price by a larger amount than the simplistic calculation — based on the assumption of unchanged quality — had led us to believe.

In the case of total spending in the economy (GNP) and the associated price (GNP deflator) the adjustment procedure is the same as that just described. However, because a quality-adjusted output number is not readily available, the procedure is more complicated. In calculating the price of total output for the economy, government divides total spending in the economy by an estimate of total output. To calculate the quality-adjusted or 'true' price of total output I divided total spending by my own estimate of total output.[13] In the case of hot chocolate mix we would have been able to use input of raw cocoa as an adjustment factor. In the case of total output, for reasons discussed below, I have used the input of labour to make the adjustment.

First, I estimated the growth rate of quality-adjusted real output (GNP). I made this estimate using a trend or normal growth rate adjusted for the quarter to quarter change in the percentage of the labor force unemployed. This procedure is derived from a well-established relationship between output and employment known as Okun's Law.[14] Since the Law is based on statistical regularity and the period of controls was not 'regular' in that sense, our estimates are subject to two sources of error. To the extent that the controls reduced union power, the relationship between output and employment imbedded in Okun's Law would tend to underestimate real output. On the other hand, shortages and administrative costs may have reduced the amount of output forthcoming from a given amount of effort and therefore the output estimate would tend to overestimate actual output. Since both of these sources of error were of trivial magnitude and offsetting in their effect on the output estimate I did not attempt to adjust Okun's Law to take them into account.

Having calculated a quality-adjusted growth rate for total output it was a simple matter to use this growth rate to calculate estimates of the level of total output and hence a quality-adjusted price of total output.

The statistical illusion

Table I — Actual and Quality-Corrected
Inflation Rates, U.S. 1970-1975

| Periods | Average Rate of Inflation | |
	Government Data	Corrected for Quality Changes
1970-I — 1971-II	5.2	5.2*
1971-III — 1972-IV	3.2	5.4
1973-I — 1974-III	9.0	7.0
1974-IV — 1975-I	11.4	11.4*
1975-II — 1975-III	5.1	5.1*

Compounded annual rates of change over previous quarter in GNP deflator (per cent per annum). Corrected data for periods not affected by the ESP (marked with asterisks) are identical to the government data.

Sources: See Figure 2.

Table 1 shows that the apparent sharp decline in the rate of inflation during Phases I and II was a statistical illusion. Indeed, the average rate of inflation corrected for quality changes rose slightly during the first six quarters of the ESP. Nor do the corrected data show such a dramatic increase in the average rate of inflation during the latter part of the control period.

Figure 2 — Reported rates of inflation compared with rates corrected for quality changes, U.S. 1970-1975

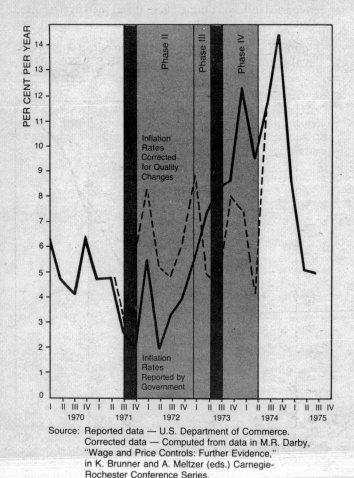

Source: Reported data — U.S. Department of Commerce.
Corrected data — Computed from data in M.R. Darby,
"Wage and Price Controls: Further Evidence,"
in K. Brunner and A. Meltzer (eds.) Carnegie-
Rochester Conference Series.

Figure 2 shows the estimates of the inflation rate corrected
for quality changes together with the inflation rate reported

in the government data. As would be expected from the detailed examination of the ESP regulations, the initial freeze involved little evasion, but the government data underreported inflation during Phase II and then overreported inflation in the succeeding Phases.

Figure 3 — Reported price level compared with price level corrected for quality changes, U.S. 1970-1975

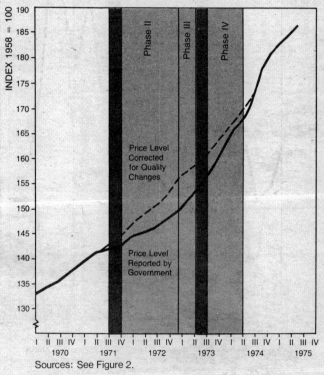

Sources: See Figure 2.

An alternative way of illustrating the effects that quality variation has on the reported price of total output is by comparing the reported and corrected estimates of the national price level. This is done in Figure 3. The difference between the reported and corrected price level represents the accumulated effect of quality degradation. This difference grows during Phase II and is thereafter reduced. The trend of the corrected price level appears little affected by the ESP.

Figure 4 — Reported growth rates of real Gross National Product compared with growth rates corrected for quality changes, U.S. 1970-1975.

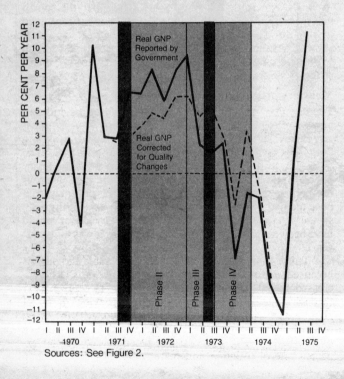

Sources: See Figure 2.

Output changes

As we saw earlier, if the assumption is made that quality has not changed, but it has in fact changed, then calculations based on that assumption will yield an overestimate of real GNP. Figure 4 compares the growth rates of real output as reported in the government data with those of the corrected data implied by Okun's Law. Figure 5 does the same for the reported and corrected estimates of the level of real GNP.

The corrected data show slower growth rates through the first quarter of 1973, and faster growth rates thereafter. Some confirmation for the correction procedure is provided by the much closer agreement of the corrected data during 1973-1974 with the behavior of such physical unit series as industrial production, employment, and railway box car loadings. These series did not seem to fall nearly as much as would be expected from the reported fall after the fourth quarter of 1973 in real GNP. Indeed, employment continued to rise through September 1974. Thus the corrected data show about the same effect from the October 1973 - March 1974 Arab oil embargo as would be expected from a major strike of similar duration.

Monetary policy during the ESP

The dominant influence on the behavior of prices and output — at least over periods of several quarters — is monetary policy. So to discover whether the (corrected) price and output behavior was different because of the ESP, it is necessary to make some assumption as to what monetary policy would have been in the absence of the ESP. There is no obvious alternative monetary policy that one may suppose the Fed would have followed in the absence of the ESP; so the discussion will assume that monetary policy would have been the same in the absence of ESP as it was in its presence.

This assumption may be unduly favorable to controls because the growth rate of the money supply was sharply increased to 8.0 per cent per annum from December 1971 through June 1973 as compared to the previous trend of about 6.0 per cent per annum. It may well be that the effect of the ESP on the reported data reduced the Fed's concern over inflation. The ESP was supposed to reduce the expected rate of inflation and hence ease the adjustment to

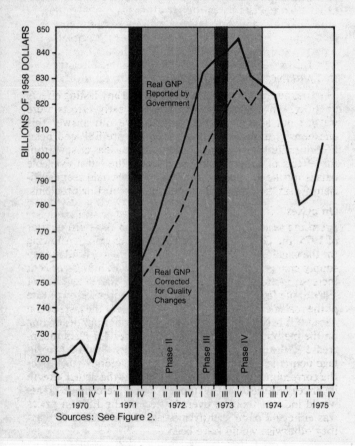

Figure 5 — Reported real Gross National Product compared with GNP corrected for quality changes, U.S. 1970-1975

Real GNP Reported by Government

Real GNP Corrected for Quality Changes

Phase II

Phase III

Phase IV

Sources: See Figure 2.

lower rates of money supply growth and inflation. Apparently the Fed did not get the message since it increased the money supply growth rate when it should have reduced it. So previous progress against inflation — achieved at a cost that included the 1969-1970 recession — was thrown away and the U.S. had to suffer another deceleration of money supply growth from July 1973 through January 1975.

V. LASTING EFFECTS OF THE ESP

The first question is whether the ESP had any lasting effects on prices and output or whether any early effects were washed out after the policy ended? We can answer this question by using government data for pre-ESP and post-ESP magnitudes with little concern about a bias arising from the effects of controls. At this writing, the latest available data is for the third quarter of 1975 which would seem sufficiently past the end of ESP to be free of reporting problems.

On prices

From the second quarter of 1971 through the third quarter of 1975, the GNP deflator rose by 31.9 per cent.[15] Allowing for the usual lag of 1.5 years for price changes behind money supply changes, this is to be compared with a 31.0 per cent increase in the money supply from the fourth quarter of 1969 to the first quarter of 1974. Now the trend growth rate of the real quantity of money demanded over the last several decades is between 0 and 0.5 per cent per annum depending on the method of calculation used. So over 4.5 years the increase in the price level should be between 0 and 2 percentage points less than the increase in the money stock over the corresponding period. So the fact that the actual growth in prices *exceeded* that of money by 0.9 percentage points would indicate that the overall effect of the ESP on prices was either nil or to slightly increase them relative to what they otherwise would have been.

On output

From the second quarter of 1971 to the third quarter of 1975 real GNP increased by 8.4 per cent.[16] However, the unemployment rate was 2.4 percentage points higher in the third quarter of 1975 than in the fourth quarter of 1971 and this had a depressing effect on output growth. In order to abstract from the effect that this change in the unemployment rate had on the growth of output, I used Okun's Law to predict what output would have been had the unemployment rate been the same. By my calculation, if the unemployment rate had not changed then real output would have risen 15.6 per cent (or 3.5 per cent per annum) had unemployment been the same. This growth rate is a bit higher than the trend growth rate of 3.1 or 3.2 per cent per annum over the last century but less than the 3.7 per cent per annum trend of the 24 postwar years before the controls. So, except to the extent that the unemployment rate in the third quarter of 1975 was influenced by the ESP, there is, in the case of output as well, no evidence of a lasting effect of the ESP.

Short-run effects of the ESP

There are no models which can consistently predict the rate of inflation in any particular quarter with an accuracy of, say, plus or minus one percentage point. Because it is difficult for us to ascertain what prices would have done in any particular quarter in the absence of controls it is correspondingly difficult to ascertain what the effect of controls was in any particular quarter. As we have just seen, this does not preclude an assessment of the overall effect, but does render difficult the assessment of particular short-run periods like Freeze I which lasted for only one quarter.

On the basis of my research I would have to conclude that the quality-adjusted price data behave very much as would be expected from the behavior of money supply growth and that controls had no discernible effect in particular quarters except in two instances:

(1) Freeze I reduced the level of prices relative to the predicted level by about 1 per cent during the third quarter of 1971 and the fourth quarter of 1971, but this was mostly caught up during the next two quarters.

(2) The very high rate of inflation during the fourth quarter of 1974 was considerably higher than would be expected but this appears to have been largely offset by the reduced rates of inflation during the second quarter of 1975 and the third quarter of 1975.

The effects of Freeze I were seen in Section II to reflect a brief increase in the number of employees who could be hired at the frozen wage because of reduced expectations of inflation. The temporary real reduction in the price level was reflected in a temporary increase in employment and real output.

The 14.4 per cent per annum rate of inflation in the fourth quarter of 1974 was about 6 percentage points higher than would be expected from past monetary policy. This anomaly may have been caused by strategic price increases due to widespread fear that controls would be reimposed and to an illusion that such price increases were possible; an illusion fostered by a naive public acceptance of the over-reported rates of inflation during the decontrol period. While this price behavior undoubtedly worsened the recession caused by the July 1973 - January 1975 deceleration of money supply growth, it is too tenuously related to be fairly attributed to the ESP.

VI. EVALUATION AND CONCLUSIONS

The major direct effect of the Economic Stabilization Program was to impart a significant bias to government price indices such as the GNP deflator; inflation was underreported during Phase II and overreported thereafter through the decontrol period. America is blessed with statistical bureaus staffed by diligent, honest civil servants who would never go along with fudging the data. The ESP's combination of arbitrary price ceilings on large firms and a tiny enforcement staff induced firms to provide 'prefudged' data to the statistical bureaus which in turn used it in all good faith to compute the price indices. Given the difficulties which these bureaus face in correcting for overt changes in quality, they can hardly be blamed for missing such covert changes.

When the data are corrected for quality changes, only Freeze I seems to have been successful at the stated goal of reducing the rate of inflation. Even that success was balanced by more rapid inflation in the next few quarters. The growth in the price level from the last pre-ESP quarter to the latest post-ESP quarter was certainly no less rapid than would have been anticipated in the program's absence. Similar, real income growth was stimulated during Freeze I, but any such effect soon washed out. So, as a means of reducing inflation and increasing real income, the ESP was a failure.

Early defenders of the ESP had argued that while the program could not reduce inflation of itself, it could ease the adjustment to a lower rate of inflation brought about by monetary policy. The idea was to reduce inflationary anticipations by a bold political stroke so that the temporary increase in employment associated with reduction of inflation rates would be moderated. Unfortunately, the Federal Reserve System instead of reducing the growth rate of the money supply significantly increased it and hence the inflation rate. This may have reflected a naive acceptance of the underreported Phase II inflation rates or simply a feeling that the ESP relieved the Federal Reserve System of responsibility for controlling the inflation rate. It is a nice question whether it is politically feasible for the central bank to continue monetary restraint after the imposition of such a program.

Phase II in effect subjected unions to regulation of their monopoly power. But the lost output due to union power is normally a trivial percentage of total output so any reduction in union power could only result in a trivial percentage gain.[17] Against this gain must be weighed the loss of output due to the administrative costs of the program and misallocated resources in the industries restrained at one time or another by controls. It would be difficult to conclude that benefits significantly exceeded the costs.

In sum, the Economic Stabilization Program was little more than a huge public relations scheme. Some were hurt, some were helped. A few quarters showed lower inflation rates than would be expected, others showed higher inflation rates. Many people still believe that Phase II was a success and if such a program were implemented without the mistakes of Phases III and IV, a controls program would be effective. This conclusion was seen to rest on biases in the data reported by the government. For little economic gain if not a small loss, people's civil rights to own property and enter into exchanges with consenting adults were limited. The resulting deterrent to future investment may well be the only important and lasting effect of the program.

Notes

[1]For a complete analysis, the interested reader should see Michael R. Darby, *Macroeconomics: The Theory of Income, Employment, and the Price Level*, New York: McGraw-Hill, 1976, especially Chapter 7.

[2]U.S. Council of Economic Advisers, *Economic Report of the President 1972*, Washington: Government Printing Office, 1972, p. 96.

[3]Low-wage employees were exempted by statute.

[4]Note that only 20 to 25 per cent of the U.S. labor force belong to unions.

[5]U.S. Council of Economic Advisers, *Economic Report of the President 1973*, Washington: Government Printing Office, 1973, p. 66.

[6]Such as 'conservative' valuation of end-of-period inventories so as to increase the reported cost of goods sold and reduce the reported net income.

[7]Workers in nonunionized firms and consumers also benefited — while owners of nonunionized firms were hurt — from the regulation of the unions' monopoly power, but the dollar amounts *per individual* in these much larger groups was much smaller than for those directly involved with unionized firms.

[8]Fifty six per cent were exempted as of July 1972 according to U.S. Cost of Living Council, *Economic Stabilization Program Quarterly Report*, Covering the Period July 1, 1972, through September 30, 1972, Washington: Government Printing Office, 1972, p. 33-34.

[9]Albert Rees, "The Effects of Unions on Resource Allocation," *Journal of Law and Economics*, October 1963, 6: 69-78. Rees estimated that there might be a similar reduction in real output because of wasteful work rules, but these were not covered by the ESP.

[10]Money demand in fact increases less than in proportion to short-run changes in output.

[11]The lumber, oil, and leather industries (accounting for a bit less than 2 per cent of gross national product) were the only ones with significantly restrictive profit margin ceilings. Evasion was nevertheless quite easy in the multiproduct and deconcentrated lumber and leather industries and added little to the consumers' cost of those products. Oil was relatively easy to control as to both price and quality and shortages of fuel oil arose.

[12]See Section III below for more detail on these estimates.

[13]By the method of calculation, growth in real GNP will be overreported to the extent that the rate of inflation is underreported; so an independent estimate is necessary.

[14]Arthur Okun, "Potential GNP: Its Measurement and Significance," *1962 Proceedings of the Business and Economic Statistics Section of the American Statistical Association*, p. 98-104.

[15]Or 6.7 per cent per annum.

[16]Or 1.9 per cent per annum.

[17]The dollar amount is nonetheless on the order of $2 billion which is not trivial in itself.

The Post-War Record

A View From The Outside
Of The Inside
Of Upside Down

JACKSON GRAYSON

*Dean, School of Business Administration
Southern Methodist University*

THE AUTHOR

Professor C. Jackson Grayson, Jr. was Chairman of the Price Commission in Phase II of President Nixon's Economic Stabilization Program. He is presently Professor and Dean, School of Business Administration, Southern Methodist University. Born in Louisiana in 1923, Dean Grayson was graduated with an M.B.A. from the University of Pennsylvania and a D.B.A. from Harvard University in 1959.

Aside from a distinguished academic career (Dean of Business at Tulane University, Professor at Stanford University, etc.), Dean Grayson has had a wide variety of working experience — having been a newspaper reporter, an FBI special agent, a consultant, a pilot, in the export-import business and a plantation manager.

Among the books he has written is *Confessions of a Price Controller* (Dow-Jones Irwin, 1974) with Louis Neeb.

The Post-War Record

A View From The Outside Of The Inside Of Upside Down

JACKSON GRAYSON

Dean, School of Business Administration
Southern Methodist University

I. INTRODUCTION

On the 18th of October, 1971, I assumed responsibility for the Price Commission in the conduct of Phase II of President Nixon's Wage and Price Control program. A detailed account of the 15 months of the program is to be found in my book with Louis Neeb, *Confessions of a Price Controller.* The purpose of this essay is not to reiterate that ground but to attempt to draw out of it lessons for the future. In the course of the essay I will draw several conclusions about wage and price controls policies that arise not from a detailed economic analysis, but from common sense reflections on my experiences during Phase II.

II. THE MAKING OF POLICY

In coming to the task of Chairman of the Price Commission I was new to the economic policy 'game' and certainly shared some of the popular delusions about the way in which the policy process worked. In particular, and without having given the matter much thought, I was under the impression that economic policy was conducted in a very precise fashion in a milieu somehow above the foibles of human nature. It is easy to understand how and why I might have had that impression. I think that the average person wants to think that somewhere somebody does know exactly what is going on and what needs to be done about it. Few people want to believe that the policy-making process is as uncertain (perhaps more so) and as subject to human frailty as the economic behavior that policy attempts to control.

In the course of the next few pages I want to relate something about my view of policy-making at the national level. I want to explain why it is inherently a confused sort of occupation and I want to imbue the reader with a healthy skepticism for the ability of central control to solve economic problems.

Information overload

One of the main reasons why the policy-making process in general and wage and price controls in particular are inherently difficult is because they are attempting to regulate the most sophisticated information system that the world has ever seen — namely the North American market economy. Information from market decisions leads to decisions that determine the production, income and spending activities that, taken together, are the economy. It tells people when to hire more (or fewer) people and machines, it tells people how much they can expect to pay for a mind-boggling menu of products, it allocates scarce resources to their most valued use, it causes new firms to come into existence and others to leave industry. It tells people where they should live and under what general conditions, and so on.

The information system is the network formed by free people buying and selling and the signals are the variations in and the levels of wages, prices, interest rates, rents and, unfortunately, taxes.

What the system does

Very often the best way to determine the contributions of people or things to an ongoing process is to see what happens in their absence. The system of price controls in the U.S. attempted, for a time, to replace the U.S. market mechanism. (I say 'attempted' because the market is like a balloon — when it is squeezed, activity simply moves in the direction of least resistance. Much evidence of legally permissible evasion of the spirit of controls was beginning to emerge early in the program.) To the extent that the program was effective, it began to produce an astonishing variety of evidence on the job that the market mechanism had been performing.

Shortages of products (ranging from natural gas to molasses) began to appear as slow-to-rise controlled prices told producers 'don't make more' and told consumers 'buy more'. Some products (fertilizer for example) were exported and sold at market prices elsewhere rather than at controlled prices within the U.S. Certain chemical derivatives of petroleum could be purchased only by bartering other chemicals in exchange. In the case of lumber products, virtually all of the classic distortions associated with price control appeared.

For example, log prices were not controlled, but the price of finished lumber was. Predictably, this led to a shortage of finished lumber, produced an array of artificial middlemen and active black markets. Ultimately, our efforts to control lumber prices led to reduced production and an increase in the export of lumber.

In short, most of the products and services that we take for granted in our everyday lives can be taken for granted only because there is a functioning price system. A system that, despite its imperfections, delivers just the right quantity of California lettuce to Montana or Alberta, Canada; and decides the relationship between raw log prices in California and the price of finished lumber in Boston. As we discovered when we tampered with, and effectively suspended, the operation of the price system, we could no longer rely on the system itself and were forced to get more and more involved with what were, before controls, essentially automatic functions.

The problem that policy-makers must cope with, if they are determined to control the system, is the endless detail that is involved in the operation of the system. To control the system and yet keep it running smoothly, the authorities must intercept all of the signals coming from the system (and there are hundreds of millions), interpret them, appropriately change them (assuming they know how) and retransmit them.

To be effective the controllers must replace the automatic aspects of the system with discretionary, centralized decisions. In point of fact, such wholesale replacement is not possible and the most that the authorities can hope to do is to influence a very few of the signals.

What a tangled web

So, there is no omniscient policy maker who knows what exactly is going on and what exactly must be done. There are only men with some understanding of how the system works and some ability to change the signals. Owing to the almost unlimited ability of the system to change and adapt, the policy-maker can never be sure that the most recent change in policy was the correct one. He can be sure, however, that it won't be the last one.

What we at the Price Commission continuously found was that everything is related to everything else and there was, accordingly, no such thing as one intervention. We were drawn inevitably and progressively deeper into the system and the temptation to limit the necessity for our involvement by arbitrarily changing the system was very great. Herein lies the real danger from centralized control, that is, that an inability to handle the overload of signals, both incoming and outgoing, may produce attempts to simplify the system and hence jeopardize its survival.

III. PRICE CONTROL POLICIES — A RELENTLESS TIDE OF DETAIL

In this section I want to discuss the important role that complexity plays in the operation of a control program. Complexity lies at the base of the difficulties that a would-be price controller faces - it manipulates the thinking of those who would design a control strategy, it frustrates the controller and his agents and ultimately it leads to the collapse of the control system. I want to spend some time on this notion because although complexity exists in every instance of central economic policy, the effects are nowhere as clear as they are in the case of wage and price controls. To that extent we can regard wage and price controls as a 'case study' in 'applied economic policy'.

Most forms of economic policy attempt to achieve a change in the course of economic activity by operating through the signalling mechanism as it exists. For example, a change in the personal tax rate reduces take home pay and thereby signals people to reduce their expenditures. Subsidies to particular industries strengthen the 'produce more' signals and encourage production that might not otherwise have occurred.

Wage and price controls, on the other hand, by design prevent the signalling mechanism from working. Ostensibly, the goal is to prevent wages and prices from increasing or to limit the rate at which they increase. In effect, however, controls eliminate the relative movements in wages and prices that do the signalling work. For example, the rise in wages in an area of the country with a labor shortage will not be allowed to occur under controls. The rise in price of particular sorts of building materials that would signal to builders to substitute other materials and signal to producers to increase their outputs of the materials in short supply will not be permitted to occur. The list of signals, under controls, that will not be transmitted in the market place is almost endless.

Life goes on

Although for a time wage and price controls can remove the flow of information in the economy, they cannot remove the functions that the information flow performs. Commodities in short supply must be rationed somehow; a shortage of skilled tradesmen must somehow be placed in the most valuable jobs. It is this sort of fact that haunts wage and price controllers, that leads to elaborate evasion schemes and that ultimately leads either to the abandonment of controls or the imposition of progressively more stringent and pervasive central control over economic activity.

Not only prices and wages

Controls on wages and prices are not just that, they are also controls on the flow of all the resources of an economy. What do I mean by that? Well, when we at the Price Commission were making decisions about the justifiability of a price increase we were effectively deciding about the value of the products involved. A decision not to allow the requested price increase on commodity A, but to allow it on commodity B, meant that we were restricting the ability of the producer of commodity A to compete for resources to use in the production of commodity A. In many cases this meant that less of commodity A was produced.

When we started Phase II we inherited from the Phase I Freeze a 400 page book of problems of industries, firms and individuals being squeezed to the point of bankruptcy, shortages and law suits when Freeze prices were set below the costs of production. There were impending shortages of products ranging from applesauce to peanut butter. Obviously, our actions to allow or not to allow price increases involved more than the rate of increase in the consumer price index.

The impossible dream

The difficulty of taking over the wage-price signalling mechanism is indicated by the fact that during the first three weeks of Phase II there were nearly 400,000 inquiries about the program. In terms of getting down to the nitty gritty, had the Dow Chemical Company and the Commission not agreed to an across the board increase of 2 per cent we would have had to examine nearly 100,000 submissions on different products for that company alone. A similar story could be told about the 1,500 largest companies with which a similar across the board average increase was negotiated. While the average increase saved the bacon in terms of the administrative burden that we had to bear, it gave the Commission less control over individual product prices since the companies could increase selected prices by as much as the market would bear. (Eventually, we had to establish a limit because of public opinion). In retrospect, though, it seems likely that this averaging provision helped the economy avoid some of the more serious distortions that wage and price controls can cause and were causing during the Phase I Freeze.

Enforcement

It is clear to me that it is in general quite impossible to literally control prices in an economy as large as that of the U.S. or Canada as long as we retain our free society. History teaches us that even in the presence of the severest form of coercion, attempts to control wages and prices have not been successful except when there has been a general support for them. Being totally honest I have to say that I don't think that our efforts in Phase II would have been successful without the whole-hearted support of the firms subject to control. Even in those cases where violations were discovered there was little evidence that there was intent to act in a manner out of keeping with the spirit of the controls.

"Is prostitution a service industry or a regulated utility?"

This, possibly tongue-in-cheek, request from a legal brothel in Nevada indicates the reason why controls cannot work in an adversary climate. The possibilities and incentive for evasion grow at an increasing rate the longer controls are in force. If there is a determination to avoid the spirit of controls, then the actual words of the control legislation and the enforcement machinery have to be extraordinarily complex. Enforcement of law in the system of justice common to free societies takes the form of a judicial procedure. Accordingly the handling of all compliance checks, including the filing of statistical evidence, has to be handled in a legally appropriate manner so that the material can be used in a court of law.

In some cases the potential size of this task precluded the Price Commission from establishing controls where they were thought to be necessary. The service industry is a good example. The Commission initially voted to put a 3 per cent ceiling on price increases in the service industry. We reversed that decision for two reasons. First of all, there are millions of service firms and the Internal Revenue Service, which was acting as our enforcement arm, didn't think they could enforce the regulation. Secondly, the staff of the Commission felt that it would not be possible to devise forms to secure data in a form proper for analysis and decision-making. In another case, we recontrolled the lumber industry only to have to back off, owing to an avalanche of paper.

The blinding light of science

People are surprised that in an age of computers and sophisticated data processing that mere operational details could be a determining factor in the control process. For example, it was suggested to me on more than one occasion that the Price Commission ought to use some of the sophisticated mathematical decision-making models that have been developed with the advent of large, high speed computers. In fact, I think that some people assumed that we were using highly-sophisticated econometric models to 'fine tune' the economy. We did look at such models, but the builders were the first to admit that these models were not useful for our purposes. In fact, there are no models of use in 'planning' a detailed control system available and my considered opinion is that they are not likely to be forthcoming in the future. I should add that I am not opposed to models and computers in principle and am a member in good standing of the Operational Research Society of America.

No escape

I have perhaps said enough by now to convince the reader that wage and price controls are, by nature, a bureaucratic nightmare. There is no easy way to proceed, no escape from the remorseless tide of detail that is the inevitable consequence of attempting to interrupt the normal current of economic affairs. There is also no escape from the conclusion that detailed regulation breeds a restiveness in those being regulated that eventually must lead either to the collapse of the controls or the adoption of more coercive measures.

IV. THE SIDE EFFECTS OF CONTROL

The wishful thinking that produces wage and price controls is the expression of a belief that controls can stop inflation. That belief is the subject of careful analysis elsewhere in this volume. Also, Professor Michael Darby has made an effort to assess the impact that the Economic Stabilization Program (ESP) of which Phase II was a part, had on the rate of inflation. Whether the program was a successful anti-inflation device or not, it certainly had the side-effects or costs and leaving to the reader to assess Professor Darby's work I want in this section to address myself to the side effects that I observed.

Equity

Our first realization in the Price Commission was that if the control system was to be manageable it had to be simple. In the face of the complexity of individual circumstances that we proposed to control we knew there would be a mismatch — we knew there would be unequal treatment of equals. But, our objective was action and the ability to act. And so our first conscious decision was to be simple and to be arbitrary.

It seems to me that inequity is an inevitable consequence of the sort of wage and price control program that we attempted to run in Phase II and which is currently being activated for Canada. In a program of this sort there isn't the time or the resources to permit the detailed regulation that equity demands.

Another sort of inequity that may be associated with controls relates to the fact that, for the majority of firms, compliance was more or less self-regulated. The chances that a small firm violating the controls would escape detection were very large. Hence those who did — and I have no doubt there were some — gained at the expense of those who did not. It is an odd law, indeed, that confers advantages on those who ignore it and punishes those who comply. We have to accept, however, that such could well have been the case.

Distortions

Another of the costs associated with controls that has been discussed in previous sections is that of the distortions that controls produce in the system. In some cases these distortions occur directly as a result of the fact that controls treat the symptoms of inflation and not its causes. For example, rising world demand for some products caused world prices for these products to rise — a phenomenon unrelated to the 'cost-push' we were trying to control. The presence of controls in the U.S. simply meant that domestic supplies were exported. The shortages that ensued were a direct consequence of controls.

In other cases the distortions arose from the attempt of firms to avoid inequities built into the controls themselves. Companies trapped by the controls with low base-period profit margins were beginning to consider selling out to companies with higher base-period margins or shipping their capital out of the country. In the case of the labor market, instances of false job upgrading — which were actually 'raises' in disguise — were reported on a scattered but increasing basis.

The security blanket effect

Perhaps the most disturbing but least obvious effect of a wage and price control program is the impact that it has on people's perceptions of, and attitudes toward, economic reality. In particular, it is my feeling that controls give people a false sense of security. They create the illusion that 'the problem is being solved' — that 'everything is under control'. The fact is, as is evident from the experiences I related above, that *the more centralized decision-making becomes, the less control is actually exercised over economic activity. Centralized decision-making cannot replace the countless millions of decisions that are made in the market automatically. The most likely effect of centralized decision-making is not more control over economic activity, but less economic activity, less productivity and in the end more inflation.*

The other aspect of controls as an instigator of a false sense of security lies in the possibility that they will distract public attention from the true causes of inflation. For example, there is some evidence that the control program in the U.S. was used as a damper to temporarily keep the lid on inflation, while the money supply was being increased at an inflationary rate. Ultimately, inflation seems to be a monetary phenomenon and is not brought under control until the growth in the money supply has been checked. *To the extent that wage and price controls permit excessive monetary expansion in the short-term, they are counter - productive and are against the public interest.*

PART III

what is
the solution?

An Alternative
To
Wage and Price Controls

DAVID LAIDLER

Professor of Economics
University of Western Ontario

THE AUTHOR

David E.W. Laidler was born in 1938 and educated at the London School of Economics, where he graduated BSc Econ with First Class Honours in 1959; the University of Syracuse (MA Economics, 1960); and the University of Chicago (PhD., 1964). After teaching (in both Britain and the U.S.A.), Professor Laidler was appointed Professor of Economics at the University of Manchester in 1969.

In 1975, Professor Laidler joined the Department of Economics at the University of Western Ontario. Professor Laidler is a member of the Editorial Advisory Board of the Fraser Institute.

Professor Laidler's publications include *The Demand for Money - Theories and Evidence*, (International Textbook Co., 1969), and *Introduction to Microeconomics*, (Philip Allan Publishers, 1974); he edited (with David Purdy) *Labour Markets and Inflation*, (Manchester University Press, 1974). With Michael Parkin, he published "Inflation: A Survey" in the December 1975 issue of the *Economic Journal*.

An Alternative To Wage and Price Controls

DAVID LAIDLER

Professor of Economics
University of Western Ontario

I. INTRODUCTION

It is all very well to argue that wage and price controls will
not work, but the fact remains that inflation in Canada is a
serious problem. It is not only harmful on the narrow
economic front but, perhaps more important from a long
run point of view, it is socially divisive as well. As yet,
Canada is far away from that state of affairs that prevails in
many Latin American countries such as Argentina (and
maybe in the U.K.) where rapid inflation poses a constant
and dangerous threat to political stability. Nevertheless, the
last three or four years have seen a small but discernible
movement in that direction. Though there is no reason for
resort to panic measures, there is every reason to take the
problem seriously. Thus, it is not sufficient to criticize the
measures that Prime Minister Trudeau took on October 13,
1975. One must also have a positive alternative to offer.

A feasible objective

In this chapter I shall set out a coherent anti-inflation policy that there is every reason to suppose would work. As we shall see, the policy in question is no panacea. It provides no guarantee of economic and social bliss. It does, however, promise a low and stable rate of inflation and with it the possibility of maintaining a reasonably high level of employment. Perhaps these goals sound modest, and compared with the claims that were made about what could be achieved with the new Keynesian economics in the post Second World War era, they are.

The policy proposals contained in this essay hinge on my judgement that the capability of Canadian economic policy to solve economic problems was badly oversold in the 1950's and 1960's. I would contend that the root of many of our current difficulties lies in having tried to achieve too much by means of these policies. That 'man's reach should exceed his grasp' is in most circumstances an admirable and desirable state of affairs. However, if the circumstance is the Federal Government's economic policy and the objective is, for example, an arbitrarily low rate of unemployment then the inflationary consequence could be disastrous. The policy advocated in the following pages has, in these terms, modest goals, but they have the great virtue of being attainable. Furthermore, the policy incorporates an explicit recognition of the fact that nobody knows precisely and in detail how the economy functions. We have too long lived with the pretense of knowledge about the economy.

The chapter is divided into two distinct sections. First, I set out the kind of economic policy that I think would produce a non-inflationary economy. Of particular concern in that discussion are the limits that pursuit of stable prices places on the pursuit of other desirable economic goals. I shall argue that there is no question of implementing such a policy immediately and that it must be approached gradually. Hence the second major section of this chapter is devoted to discussing the problems involved in making the transition from the present inflationary situation to a situation of long-run price stability.

The return to a low inflation rate will not be achieved without cost; a cost measured in terms of the economic and social dislocation associated with unemployment. However, I do not believe that there is any alternative to the measures I am proposing here that has any hope of success in curing inflation at less cost to Canadians. I am not describing below one out of a number of equally attractive alternative strategies that may be used to deal with inflation. Rather I am advocating what might best be called the least unattractive of the policies available to deal with Canada's present problems; a policy, however, which is much more attractive than the alternative of continuing and perhaps accelerating double- digit inflation with all that that implies.

II. THE PROGRAMME

Objective: a constant cost of living?

The first step in designing policy to produce a non-inflationary economy is to set a reasonable and attainable goal. It is impossible to achieve a state of affairs in which the cost of living for each and every member of the community remains constant on a day by day or even year by year basis. Even if the cost of living as measured by, say, the consumer price index were to be held constant over time, some members of the community would find their own cost of living varying, perhaps up or perhaps down, at any particular time. For instance, the relatively poor spend a larger proportion of their incomes on food than do the rich. A bad harvest would tend to push up the price of food even against a background of overall price stability, and would cause the cost of living of the relatively poor to increase. On the other hand, the relatively rich spend a greater proportion of income on travel. A worsening of the energy situation would tend to make the costs of travel rise relative to other prices and hence face the rich with an increase in their cost of living.

The inflation target

There is no way of preventing things like bad harvests and changes in the world price of oil and it is therefore idle to pretend that everyone can be guaranteed a constant cost of living.† What can be done, however, is to follow policies that will ensure that overall, taking one year with another, the inflation rate will vary about a constant rate close to zero. The rate of inflation that existed in the early 1960's (about 2 per cent per year) before economic policy was set on an inflationary course, would be a realistic and attainable goal.

The central role of money

It has been demonstrated in earlier chapters that the long-term path of inflation is overwhelmingly governed by the relative rates of production of goods and money. If the total supply of money is expanding at some rate faster than the total supply of things that money can buy, then inflation is the inevitable consequence; a fact recognized by conventional wisdom in the saying 'too many dollars chasing too few goods'.

Although too much can be made of this old 'saw', we can say that long-run stability in the inflation rate would be achieved if the Bank of Canada adopted a policy of making the supply of money in the Canadian economy grow at some constant rate year in and year out. The resulting inflation rate would also be low if the increase in the money supply were equal to the rate at which the economy is increasing its output of goods.[1] This, in a nutshell, is the reason for my proposal that we establish a rule to regulate the rate at which money can be created by the Federal Department of Finance.‡ Such a policy rule would 'work' because of the well-established relationship between the money supply and total spending to which we now turn.

---

†Editor's Note: The Canadian government attempted, for a time, to maintain the price of oil in Canada at a level lower than the world price. This policy will be abandoned in 1976 because Canada could not afford to follow this policy.

‡Editor's Note: Although the Bank of Canada is responsible for the day to day conduct of monetary policy, it does not have independent decision-making powers about the central thrust of that policy. This point was firmly established in the confrontation in 1961 between James Coyne, then Governor of the Bank of Canada, and the then Minister of Finance, Donald Fleming.

The households, firms, and other institutions that make up the economy use money — currency and bank deposits — to carry on their everyday business. The amount that any individual will require to keep on hand on average depends upon the volume of purchases and sales that he is involved in and the average price at which these transactions takes place. The amount that the average family decides to keep will depend on its circumstances and preferences. Budget-conscious families would probably keep a close correspondence between the average balance and the minimum required. Families less conscious of their day-to-day finances would tend to have a cash position that varied between too much and not enough during a given short period. Typically, a family maintains its cash position via weekly or bi-monthly receipt of salary (cash) payments.

It turns out that the collective result of individuals and firms trying to maintain their holdings of money at a convenient level is that there exists a stable relationship in the economy as a whole between total national spending and the amount of money that the economy requires to carry on its business. The existence of such a relationship for an enormous variety of times and places, including the contemporary Canadian economy, is one of the best established facts of applied economics.[2]

I referred to this relationship as stable, not as constant. The relationship between money holding on the one hand and real expenditure and prices on the other is not one that can be readily observed on a day by day or even quarter by quarter basis. It is one that exists, on average, on a year by year basis. Roughly speaking, the economy's requirement for money increases in proportion to real expenditure and in proportion to the price level. Thus, if the Bank of Canada permits money to be produced at the same rate that the economy is increasing the output of goods, then that will accommodate people's desire to hold money only if the prices of goods remain constant.

How the system adjusts

In order to see how the relationship between money and inflation works, let us suppose that the price level did not remain constant. Suppose that because of some outside or 'exogenous' influence, like the oil shortage, prices started to increase. What would happen then? At first, interestingly, nothing very much would happen. People would find themselves temporarily short of cash, as they tried to carry on the same volume of business at a higher price level. One would not expect them to take immediate action in response to this because although a cash shortage is inconvenient, it is not something that requires instantaneous attention. Most people and corporations have access to short-term credit facilities of either a formal or informal sort. Formal short-term credit facilities are provided by a variety of financial institutions and credit card companies. Informal credit facilities are often provided by simply putting off the payment of a bill — often at a penalty.

The day of reckoning can only be postponed for a short while, however, and as a cash shortage persists, we can expect people and firms to begin to take action to build their cash holdings up to a more comfortable level. How they will do this will depend upon particular individuals. Some will temporarily cut back on expenditures in order to let cash build up; others will try to dispose of other assets that they are holding, such as savings deposits, bonds, or stocks; while others will attempt to extend their credit from banks and other financial institutions.

All this activity will put upward pressure on interest rates, which in turn will have two further effects. First of all, it will encourage people to synchronize their expenditures more closely with their incomes because of the loss involved in unproductive (no yield) cash holdings. This effect is probably much smaller for individuals than it is for firms simply because of the dollar amount of the cash holdings involved. In any event, given the higher cost of borrowing or the higher amount of interest foregone people, on average, will be slow to adjust their cash back to the accustomed pre-squeeze position.[3]

Secondly, and of crucial importance, higher interest rates will also begin to impinge on postponable spending decisions — particularly perhaps the investment decisions of firms, as well as households' decisions about purchases of durable goods — housing, automobiles, furniture and such. Overall pressure will build up for expenditures to fall which will in turn work against the forces that were tending to push prices up in the first place and ultimately cancel them out.

Conversely, any initial tendency for prices to fall will, if the production of money proceeds at a constant percentage rate, be met by the emergence of excess cash holdings as, temporarily, cash receipts exceed cash expenditures. This excess will produce a tendency for interest rates to fall and demand to expand, thus putting upward pressure on prices. In short, if the production of money proceeds at a constant growth rate, compatible with the performance of the economy, this will act as a powerful 'built-in stabilizer' to the economy, tending to maintain price stability without any direct action on the part of the authorities. This will not guarantee complete stability, but on average, taking one year with another, the inflation rate will not deviate far from zero if such a policy 'rule' is maintained.

Fine tuning

But the question must immediately arise as to whether we cannot iron out the remaining fluctuations as well. For instance, when prices begin to rise, why not actively slow down the rate of increase in the money stock to speed up the return to price stability? In principle there can be no doubt that this is possible — but problems arise in practise. It requires a great deal of knowledge of what is happening in the economy, and of what is going to happen, to know by just how much and for how long to apply such a countervailing policy. There is always the danger that fine tuning will end up putting on too much pressure in the opposite direction or in putting on pressure at the wrong time. If it does, such an active policy, however well-intentioned, would produce less price stability over time than would be achieved by forcing the money supply to grow at a constant rate. There is considerable doubt as to whether we have enough knowledge of the structure of the Canadian economy to be able appropriately to vary the money supply as a means of stabilizing the economy without thereby doing more harm than good. If there is such doubt then prudence dictates that we settle for a constant growth rate in the money supply — i.e. a money supply rule. Its implementation will not ensure perfection, but it will produce a state of affairs much to be preferred to the one we now find ourselves in.

Money is . . .

We have carried on the foregoing discussion on the understanding that we know exactly what we mean by 'money'. We have referred to it as 'currency in circulation with the public plus the volume of bank deposits' but which deposits and at which banks? Deposits are not all alike. Clearly chequing deposits at Chartered Banks are very similar to currency and everyone would agree to treat them as money. But what about savings deposits at Chartered Banks, and what about chequable deposits with Trust Companies and Credit Unions? Does it make any difference which deposits are included and excluded from the quantity of 'money' that the Bank of Canada is supposed to control?

The reader will not be suprised to learn that the most appropriate way for defining the 'money stock' in the Canadian economy is a matter of controversy even among economists. However, that controversy is not central to the issues under discussion here. Although different classes of bank deposits are capable of growing at quite divergent rates for periods of months or more, over longer time spans different definitions of money, that include different classes of deposits, behave with considerable similarity. There is every reason to believe that, if the behaviour of one definition of money was tied down by a rule, this factor would impart sufficient stability to the monetary sector so that other definitions would also grow in a stable fashion over time. There is, however, some risk that if a very narrow definition was chosen, there might be room for an uncomfortable amount of slippage in the system, and so I would prefer to see the growth rule applied to a rather broad definition of money — one that included savings deposits at Chartered Banks and chequable deposits at such institutions as Trust

Companies, but which excludes large scale non-chequable term deposits. Even so, there is nothing in the case for adopting a monetary growth rate rule that hinges critically upon the choice of one specific definition of money rather than another over quite a broad class of alternatives.

III. LIMITATIONS ON OTHER POLICIES

Monetary policy is not carried on in a vacuum. It is but one of the tools available to any federal or central government, and cannot be implemented independently of them. The government may manipulate its expenditure and taxes, but such fiscal measures interact with monetary policy, as does policy towards the exchange rate. The implementation of a rule for the rate of growth of the money supply puts constraints upon the use of these other tools which we must now discuss.

On fiscal policy

Let us begin with government fiscal policy — i.e. taxation and expenditure policy. Any government, federal or provincial, must balance its books. It must cover its expenditure either from taxes or by borrowing — or, additionally, in the case of provincial governments with grants from the federal government. In the present context, it is the federal government that is important, because one source from which it can borrow is the Bank of Canada. When it does that, it is to all intents and purposes 'printing' money. When the Bank of Canada lends to the Federal Government it adds a government 'I.O.U.' to its assets and creates a brand new I.O.U. of its own, a Bank of Canada deposit which it hands over to the government. The government then spends this deposit, thus putting newly-created 'money' into circulation, but it is money of a special type. Bank of Canada deposits are held by the banking system as the 'back up' or reserves for the deposits that they hold for people and firms. (In earlier time the reserves were held in the form of gold). Since the banks are only required to hold one dollar of reserves for every eight to twelve dollars of deposits any increase in reserves enables the banking system as a whole to expand its deposits and hence the money supply by a multiple of that original increase.

The implication of the last paragraph is straightforward. If the Bank of Canada is to be told to ensure that the money supply grows at a constant rate year in year out, the volume of federal government borrowing from the Bank of Canada must be consistent with the pursuit of that policy. It must not fluctuate too much from year to year and can in the long run grow in volume only at about the same proportional rate at which it is intended that the money supply grow.†

The how and the whether of government spending

Now of course the government of any country, Canada included, has many other policy goals to pursue in addition to that of controlling inflation. 'National defence' must be provided for, 'health and welfare' programmes must be financed, relatively 'depressed regions' of the country might be thought to require support and subsidies, as might particular depressed industries. One can argue the merits of any particular government programme, or indeed, on a more fundamental level debate the principles upon which any form of government intervention in economic life ought to be based. However, critical though these matters are, their resolution is immaterial as far as the current discussion is concerned. The implementation of a rule for money supply growth to control inflation puts constraints on the way in which government expenditure can be financed, but not upon its overall level and structure. Such a policy is neutral as far as questions concerning the appropriate degree of government intervention in the economy are concerned.

---

†Editor's Note: An additional complication arises from the fact that the Bank of Canada acts as the agent of the Federal government when the government wants to borrow from the general public or financial institutions. In its capacity as agent for the government the Bank of Canada tries to sell all of the bonds that the government wants to issue. The banks are the principal buyers of these bonds, and often as not, the Bank of Canada makes it easy for the chartered banks to buy the government bonds by increasing the reserves that are made available to the banks. This has the effect of increasing the money supply but is not as obvious as direct borrowing from the Bank of Canada.

Hidden taxation

Nevertheless, the implementation of such a rule would require the vast majority of government programmes to be tax-financed or paid for from the proceeds of bond sales to the public. Taxes depress private spending, as do bond sales since they put upward pressure on interest rates, but that is exactly what is required, if government expenditure is to be expanded without putting undue inflationary pressures on the economy. If government spending is to be expanded in an economy operating in the region of capacity output, then private spending has to be reduced in order to make way for it. It is always politically easier for a government to increase its expenditure than to increase taxes or set in motion policies that force interest rates up. Hence there is always a strong temptation to end up borrowing from the Bank of Canada, thus effectively hiding from the population the true costs of government expenditure programmes with all that that implies.

In any event, the private sector still has to surrender some of its claims to the productive power of the nation to the government in such circumstances. Inflation resulting from excessive demands being put upon the country's resources is the means by which this surrender is accomplished when government expenditure is financed by borrowing from the Bank of Canada. The implementation of a rule for the growth rate of the money supply would force the government to act in such a way that the costs of its expenditure plans are made readily apparent to the public who one way or another must bear them. This is but another aspect of the way in which such a rule would act as an effective anti-inflationary device.

On exchange rate policy

So far, we have carried on our discussion as if we were dealing with a 'closed economy', an economy that is not involved in trade with the rest of the world or in world-wide financial markets. But Canada is deeply involved in the world economy and, being small in relation to that world economy, is potentially vulnerable to external disturbances. Let us now see what constraints the implementation of a monetary rule would place upon the economy's ability to cope with such external disturbances.

Adherence to a rule governing the rate of growth of the money supply will leave Canada with no choice but to allow exchange rate flexibility in order to cope with economic disturbances coming from elsewhere in the world. Acceptance of the implications of such a proposition is probably easier to achieve in Canada than in virtually any other western country, for Canadians have proved far less prone than others to insist on a guarantee of exchange rate stability. Nevertheless there are potential problems here, as we shall see in a moment, once we have discussed the reasons why exchange rate flexibility is so essential. It is convenient to do this by way of an example.

Let us consider what would happen if Canada were pursuing a monetary rule designed to produce a low rate of inflation at a time when there were strong inflationary pressures at work in the United States. Suppose that Canada tried to maintain a constant exchange rate between the Canadian and U.S. dollars under such circumstances. Then the prices of goods imported from the United States would begin to rise in Canada while Canadian exporters would find it easier to sell their products in U.S. markets and perhaps to raise their prices both there and at home. There would develop simultaneously a balance of payments surplus and a tendency towards domestic inflation in Canada. A constant rate of monetary expansion might cope with the tendency towards inflation but the key question is whether the rate of growth of the money supply could be maintained constant in the face of a fixed exchange rate and a balance of payments surplus. The answer here is that it almost certainly could not be, for the following reasons.

A balance of payments surplus involves the inhabitants of Canada being recipients of a net inflow of foreign currency, as foreigners buy more from Canadians than Canadians buy from foreigners. There is no reason to suppose that they will wish to accumulate and hold stocks of foreign exchange; instead they will present them to their banks in exchange for domestic currency, and the banks in turn will present the foreign exchange to the Bank of Canada for redemption. The maintenance of a fixed exchange rate requires that the Bank of Canada be willing to buy foreign exchange presented to it in unlimited amounts and at a fixed price. It buys such foreign exchange with newly-created liabilities, with newly-created money. Thus, under a fixed exchange rate, a balance of payments surplus leads automatically to a step up in the rate at which the Bank of Canada expands the money supply in just the same way as does government borrowing from the Bank of Canada.

Short-circuiting

It is sometimes thought that such a consequence can be avoided by so called 'sterilization' operations, whereby after purchasing foreign exchange the Bank of Canada sells government bonds on the open market in order to reduce the money supply again, leaving the overall quantity of money unaffected by the balance of payments surplus. The problem here is that such bond sales put upward pressure on interest rates, and this leads to an inflow of foreign capital. Such an inflow in turn increases the balance of payments surplus and hence puts further upward pressure on the rate of monetary expansion. Sterilization policies can at best delay, but cannot offset, the influence of a balance of payments surplus on the rate of production of money. The maintenance of a fixed exchange rate would make it impossible for Canada to maintain a rule for the rate of money production in the face of inflation in the United States; it would ensure that Canada would end up importing inflation from the U.S.

Free the dollar

The remedy in such circumstances is clear-cut: let the exchange rate float upwards in the face of inflationary pressures coming from abroad. Do not oblige the Bank of Canada to buy foreign currencies in unlimited amounts at a fixed price; rather leave it free to pursue a monetary rule. There is, however, one implication of such a policy that needs to be recognized. Though Canada has adopted exchange rate flexibility for a large proportion of the post-war period, there does seem to have been some kind of presumption that fluctuations in the exchange rate should be around a long-run average value of 1 dollar Canadian per dollar U.S. If both the U.S. and Canada adopt rules for monetary expansion that lead to a stable long-run inflation rate in each country that is to all intents and purposes the same, then such an average value for the exchange rate can be maintained. However, if they do not, and Canada wishes to maintain an inflation rate that is lower than that prevailing in the U.S. then it must be prepared to see the Canadian dollar appreciate indefinitely. Conversely, if the United States pursues a policy that leads to a lower inflation rate than that generated by the pursuit of a monetary rule in Canada, then the Canadian dollar will depreciate slowly but steadily and must be permitted to do so if the rule is to be adhered to.

On ability to limit capital inflows

One other aspect of the openness of the Canadian economy is particularly relevant in the current context and needs some discussion: namely, the matter of capital inflows from the United States. Such inflows are a sensitive political issue in Canada but policy towards them is intimately connected with the questions about the level of government expenditure and the means adopted to finance it discussed above. The higher the level of government expenditure in Canada, and the more of it that is financed by bond sales, the more upward pressure there will be on interest rates as funds are diverted from investment in the private sector to financing government activities. Such upward pressure on interest rates will attract investment from abroad, particularly from the United States, as funds flow in to make good the shortfall of domestic savings available to finance investment in the private sector of the Canadian economy.

If such a capital inflow is not desired, then the usual way of dealing with it, i.e. forcing down Canadian interest rates until investment in Canada is no longer attractive, is not available when a monetary rule is being pursued. It is only by increasing the rate of monetary expansion that the Bank of Canada is able to drive down interest rates. This is not to say that a capital inflow from the United States is made inevitable by the adoption of a monetary rule, nor is it to argue that such an inflow is either desirable or undesirable. It is, however, to argue that the adoption of a rule for the rate of monetary expansion puts limits on the extent to which the government can, if it so wishes, combat such an inflow.

A cut in the scale of government expenditure and a switch from bond finance to taxation as a means of funding such expenditures are the only policies available to push down domestic interest rates once a rule is adopted. Once monetary policy is fully-committed to controlling the rate of inflation it cannot also be used to pursue other policy goals. Though there is room for debate about what choice should be made between the scale of government expenditures and the amount of capital inflow that should be permitted, it is not my purpose here to take sides in such a debate; the only aim is to make it clear that, once a monetary rule is put into operation, such a choice may have to be made.

IV. THE EMPLOYMENT TARGET

Up to now we have discussed the effects of the adoption of a fixed rate of monetary expansion on exchange rate policy, policy towards the financing of government expenditure, and have referred in passing to a number of other policy goals. We have not said a word about policy towards unemployment, and yet there are many who would regard the maintenance of full employment as at least as important as the control of inflation and some who would regard it as even more important. What therefore would the implementation of a monetary rule do to the government's ability to pursue a full employment policy?

The first and obvious thing to be said is that if monetary policy is being geared towards the control of inflation, it cannot also be used actively to pursue high employment. However, this does not mean that the adoption of a monetary rule has no side effects on the unemployment rate. There is every reason to suppose that such side effects would occur and would be beneficial.

The reason for this has already in effect been discussed. A monetary rule provides built-in stability to the economy. We have sketched out above the way in which it would tend to damp down any fluctuations in the inflation rate arising from exogenous shocks, but it would work in a similar way on unemployment.[4] A downturn in the level of real expenditure and employment in an economy where a monetary rule was being pursued would automatically produce excess cash in the private sector. This would happen because, although the rate of increase in the production of goods had fallen, the money rule would maintain money production at the old rate. Hence, since the need for money has fallen but the supply has not, people on average will find that their cash position is improving. This increase in liquidity in turn would stimulate spending and hence help to return the economy to full employment.

Of course there is no reason to suppose that the stabilizing effects of the monetary rule would, by themselves, be sufficient to ensure the maintenance of a comfortable level of employment at all times. They might be, but in the present state of knowledge, there can be no guarantee. However, monetary weapons are not the only ones available to deal with unemployment. Fiscal policies involving variations in the scale of taxation and government expenditure are also there to be used to this end.

And fiscal policy too

Fiscal policies impinge directly upon the flows of income and expenditure in the economy, and it is generally agreed that they can, for that reason, have a rapid impact upon the level of employment. There is no reason to argue that the implementation of a rule for the rate of growth of the money supply should be accompanied by the abandonment of such policies. One can easily conceive of fiscal policy being used to help iron out some of the fluctuations in income and employment that would remain even when a monetary rule was providing a background of long-term built-in stability to the economy. There is one vital proviso here: any deficits in the federal budget that arise from the use of government expenditure and tax rates as stabilization devices must be covered by borrowing from the public and not by borrowing from the Bank of Canada. Only if this principle is followed can the conduct of fiscal stabilization policy be made consistent with the continuation of a constant rate of monetary expansion.[5]

It has been noted that fiscal policies act upon the economy rather quickly, and so they do *once they have been implemented.* How much one can expect of them in practise therefore depends first of all upon the speed with which the authorities recognize the need to implement them, and second upon the speed with which decisions about appropriate policies can be taken and acted upon within the government machinery. It is no good having available a policy device that can have an important impact on unemployment levels within a six month period if it takes a year to recognize the need for its use and to get it into action. Such problems, though they by no means imply that we should give up any hope of successfully using fiscal policy as a stabilization device, nevertheless ought to make us cautious in the expectations we form about what such policies can in fact accomplish.

Full employment is . . .

For the last few pages, we have been discussing the problem of maintaining full employment without actually stopping to consider what we mean by the term. Given that we don't mean a state of affairs in which every member of the labour force has a job at all times, just what is a reasonable target to pursue on the employment front? As with defining the goals towards which anti-inflation policy should aim, so when it comes to defining unemployment, it is important to have targets that are in fact attainable with the workable policies available. A growing economy is inevitably going to be in a perpetual state of flux. New products and processes are continually being introduced and the structure of output best suited to meet the desires of the population is always changing. It is an inevitable corollary of this that some industries will be shrinking, and that the labour which they are releasing must move into newer, expanding sectors of the economy.

One cannot expect such transfers of labour to take place instantaneously. At best it takes time for a worker displaced in one industry or firm to find a job elsewhere even when the change of employment requires that he acquire no new skills. When the market for a man's skills shrinks with the industry in which he is initially employed, the process of moving between jobs takes even longer. And of course it is not just existing members of the labour force moving between jobs that generates some unemployment even at the best of times. When the young enter the labour force for the first time they too must find employment, and again, one would expect that to take time, time during which they are unemployed.

A realistic goal

When we talk, therefore, of trying to achieve 'full employment' in the economy, we must allow for the consequences of structural change and frictions in the labour market in setting our goal.[6] If fifteen per cent of the labour force changed jobs each year, and on average took four months to find new employment, that alone would generate an unemployment rate of 5 per cent at any time. One might regard such unemployment as tolerable, or one might not; if one did not, it would be inappropriate to attempt to reduce it by resort to 'full employment pump priming' fiscal policies of the orthodox type discussed above. Such policies are well-adapted to dealing with unemployment that arises from a shortfall in the overall level of demand below the economy's productive potential, but extremely ill-adapted to dealing with problems whose major source is friction in the labour market.

The appropriate policies to deal with unemployment arising from labour market frictions and structural change in the economy involve reducing those frictions — making it easier for workers made redundant by technological change to acquire new skills, making it easier for people to move from labour surplus to labour shortage areas of the economy, or for industry to move in the opposite direction. There is no space in this chapter to set out and debate the merits of particular policies designed to deal with these problems. The important point in the present context is that, though the adoption of a monetary rule to deal with inflation eliminates the possibility of using monetary policy as an active anti-unemployment device, there are plenty of other policies available to government for dealing with unemployment. The implementation of such policies should in no way be inhibited by the use of such a rule except to the extent that it puts limits on the manner in which their costs are financed. Thus their merits and demerits can be debated virtually independently of the policy proposals being advanced here.

V. RECAPPING THE PROPOSAL

To sum up the argument so far: the adoption of a constant rate of growth of the money supply as the rule for the conduct of monetary policy will confer upon the economy, not perfect price stability or perpetual full employment, but a good prospect of achieving low and reasonably stable inflation and a level of employment that fluctuates around an average that may or may not be regarded as satisfactory. Remaining fluctuations in the unemployment rate may be tackled with fiscal policy but not too much should be expected in this regard. As to the average level of unemployment, if this is judged to be undesirably high, then it may be reduced with policies designed to smooth out the working of the labour market.

The adoption of this policy package does place certain constraints on the government's actions in other respects. In particular the adoption of a monetary rule implies acceptance that the great bulk of government expenditure be tax financed or paid for by borrowing from the public. It also implies that the exchange rate be allowed to find its own level, whatever that may be. These proposals stop far short of guaranteeing perfection, but they do promise a state of affairs that most of us would prefer to the current situation. However, an issue of overriding importance has been ignored so far. How are we to manage the transition from the present situation to this more desirable state of affairs? Is it in fact possible 'to get there from here'? And if it is possible, what are the costs to be borne along the way? It is to these questions that I now turn.

VI. HOW TO GET FROM HERE TO THERE

The starting point

The centrepiece of the policy package advocated in this chapter is the maintenance of a rate of growth of the money supply compatible with steady real growth and price stability. In concrete terms, that rate of monetary expansion would be perhaps four or five per cent per annum. Over the last two or three years the actual rate of growth of the Canadian money supply has been in the region of fifteen to twenty per cent. Given such a starting point, there can be no question of getting to the target rate of monetary expansion quickly, and therefore no question of bringing down the rate of inflation quickly. Policy to bring the inflation rate down needs to be conceived of in terms of years rather than months; indeed, it is far from clear that even the three year horizon currently adopted by the government for its program is in fact long enough. Let us first of all discuss the reasons why policy needs to be implemented slowly and then go on to discuss what these reasons imply for the other measures that ought to be undertaken during a period of transition to a lower inflation rate.

Expectations and inflation

The key factor to be understood here is the role that 'expectations' play in the conduct of economic activity, and in particular the role that they play in the inflationary process.[7] It is a commonplace, but an important one, that economic activity occurs over time. Decisions taken today are decisions about the future, and that future is inevitably uncertain. A firm deciding upon its production plans and its pricing policies for the future must take a view about what amounts of output it can sell and at what prices. In negotiating a wage contract both sides must base their bargaining positions, and the ultimate settlement, upon what they think are the prospects for the particular industry they are involved in, and for the economy as a whole, over the period of the contract.

The behaviour of the general price level over time and expectations about it, are pervasive elements in all economic decisions. If a wage contract is being negotiated for a one or two year period, what is settled on is the time path of money wages and fringes over that period. However, what that wage bargain means in terms of the real living standards of the wage earners affected by it depends on what happens to prices over the same period. Their negotiating representatives must form expectations about the inflation rate in order to be able to bargain rationally. But such expectations are equally important from the employer's point of view. What a particular wage agreement means to the profitability of his enterprise depends upon the prices he can expect to get for his output over the period of the contract; although this will in part be affected by conditions particular to the industry in which he is operating, it will also be heavily influenced by the behaviour of the general price level.

The self-fulfilling prophesy

Currently-held expectations about the future inflation rate thus influence currently-made decisions, including decisions about the time path of wages and prices in the future. To give a simple example; if a particular group of employers and employees are settling on a particular time path for money wages, they will presumably settle for a higher rate of increase if they expect ten per cent inflation rather than five per cent. This would happen partly because employees would want such an extra rate of wage increase to compensate them for the expected extra increase in their living costs. However, the employers in question would also expect to be able to increase their output prices at a five percentage point more rapid rate and hence would be willing to concede the higher rate of money wage increase.

This, of course, is to argue that there is a strong element of self-fulfilling prophesy about inflation. Suppose that employers and employees in all industries expect the general rate of inflation to run at ten per cent per annum. Then what? They will set their wage and price policies on that assumption, and those very policies will help to generate the inflation that was expected in the first place. But what would happen if total spending in the economy was not expanding fast enough to permit the economy to operate at full employment output with prices rising at ten per cent per annum? Suppose the rate of monetary expansion would permit only a five per cent inflation rate at full employment. The main short-term consequence of this would not be a fall in the inflation rate, but instead a downturn in real activity and an increase in unemployment.

The unemployment consequence of wage contracts

This reduction in output and employment would happen for two inter-related reasons. First, when any individual firm experiences a fall-off in sales, the managers of the firm have to decide whether such a fall is a temporary aberration which can safely be ignored, or whether it portends a longer-term shift in the market conditions that the firm faces. It takes time to gather the information necessary to make such a decision. The initial reaction to falling sales across the economy is thus a buildup of inventories of unsold goods and not much else. Only when it becomes apparent to firms that the fall in question is not a transitory phenomenom can they be expected to take action. Such action can either involve cutting prices to try to boost sales, cutting output, or a combination of such policies. The general presumption must be that the initial response will be more heavily weighted to the side of cutting output. Partly this is because it is often cheaper for firms to cut output than to go to the expense of revamping their prices and informing customers about this. Far more important, wage contracts already entered into put a severe limit on the extent to which prices can be lowered without involving the firm in losses. It is easier to cut output, put workers on short time, or lay them off altogether than to renegotiate a wage contract while it is in force, particularly when the renegotiation is in a downward direction.

The fact that inflationary expectations become imbedded in one to two year contracts complicates the response of firms to changes in the demand for their product. A declining demand for a product might be expected to lead to a reduction in its price but the fact that labour costs cannot usually be cut by changing the contract wage effectively rules out a price cut in the short run. This contractual inertia in money wage rates and hence in prices means that a downturn in total spending will be reflected in a fall in employment as firms attempt to cut their costs by laying off workers.

The bigger the downturn, the more unemployment will be generated. Until very recently the time path of the Canadian money supply has been compatible with a rate of inflation of ten per cent or more. Such an inflation rate has been widely expected, and that expectation has been built into many wage contracts. Suddenly to shift to a policy compatible with zero inflation would certainly lead to a terrible depression. An indication of the severity of such a downturn can be had in the 1970 experience discussed in Jack Carr's essay above.

A large scale downturn in the volume of spending and employment would certainly bring the inflation rate down. Inflationary expectations are only one ingredient of wage and price setting behaviour. The appearance of excess capacity in the economy would lead to firms revising their prices downward relative to initial plans (which is not the same thing as actually cutting prices in terms of dollars and cents; it might simply involve increasing prices by less than was initially intended). The unemployment associated with a depression in the level of real economic activity would similarly put downward pressure on the time path of wages. As wage contracts came up for renewal employers would not be willing to grant money wage increases at the old rate while labour force representatives would be less willing to press for such increases. The inflation rate would begin to slow down, and, as it became clear that it was indeed slowing down, expectations about the future inflation rate would in turn be revised downwards. More modest expectations of inflation would then encourage a further slowing down of inflation. In short, the shock of a sudden downturn in the economy would set in motion a cumulative reduction in the inflation rate, a reduction that would go on until the inflation rate was low enough to be compatible with the monetary policy being pursued.[8] Then, and only then, could it be expected that the economy would have returned to full employment.

Can we survive the cure?

The problem with all this, however, is that most of us would regard the cure to be at least as bad, or perhaps even worse, than the disease. If a depression along 1930 lines was the only way of getting to grips with inflation in Canada, then the alternative of living with inflation forever would begin to look attractive. Fortunately, there is no reason to suppose that these two bleak alternatives are the only ones available. A deep depression is a relatively quick cure for inflation, but if we settle for a more slow-moving treatment of the disease, we can expect to get rid of it with less pain — but not painlessly, let it be stressed.

Gradualism, but now

There is no fundamental qualitative difference between a slow cure for inflation and the quick one we have just discussed. The essence of that slow cure is to apply the same remedy more gently. Instead of going immediately from a rate of monetary expansion compatible with a ten per cent inflation rate to one that will ultimately lead to stable prices, it is possible to spread out the transition over time to slow down the rate of monetary expansion gently instead of suddenly. The longer the transition in question the longer would it be before inflation ceased to be a problem, but the less acute would be the unemployment encountered in the interim. We can get rid of inflation quickly by generating a lot of unemployment over a relatively short period — a couple of years, say — or slowly by generating a lower unemployment rate over a long period. It would help if one could offer precise quantitative estimates of the alternative time paths for inflation and unemployment envisaged here, but in the present state of knowledge it would be dangerous to pretend to any precision. My own guess, and it is a guess, is that if we set about reducing the rate of monetary expansion over a five year period to a level compatible with price stability, then we probably would not see any significant increase in unemployment above its present level. Let us now consider the way in which a slow cure for inflation will work through the system.

How the cure would work

It was argued earlier that inflation generates its own momentum, and we identified two interacting sources of that momentum, namely expectations and long-term contracts. A gentle slowdown in the rate of money production will at its inception have to press down against that momentum. It is bound to generate some excess capacity in the economy but the more gentle the slowdown the less the downward pressure of demand and the less excess capacity will be generated over any given time period. Thus, the less unemployment will there be when, at any time after the inception of the policy, wage contracts come up for renewal. Such unemployment as exists will, however, still put some downward pressure on the outcome of new negotiations, and the resulting slowdown in inflation will in turn feed into expectations. Exactly the same kind of cumulative reduction in the inflation rate as we considered above will begin to evolve, although at a slower rate.

There is one implicit assumption in the foregoing argument that is of considerable importance to our description of the process whereby the inflation rate slows down, but it is an assumption which is open to doubt. It is namely that expectations of inflation *only* get revised downwards when people *actually observe* the inflation rate falling. According to our account of the process, unemployment generates an initial slowdown in the inflation rate which in turn feeds into expectations. Now it is one thing to argue that past experience is an important factor influencing expectations and quite another to argue that it is the sole ingredient. If the government were to announce beforehand a policy of slowly reducing the money supply expansion rate in order to reduce inflation, and if it were then seen to implement and stick to such a policy, this in itself could be expected to exert a downward pressure on expectations; it would hence contribute to a slowdown in the inflation rate in a way that did not require the appearance of unemployment to bring it about. The stronger is the belief in the government's intention, the less unemployment will be required to achieve any given speed of reduction in the inflation rate.

If the government acts slowly but consistently, and above all publicly, to implement an anti-inflation policy of the type we have described here, it is too much to hope that the transition to price stability would be painless. However, such actions would give Canada its best chance of getting rid of inflation at minimum cost — or at least the best chance that is available in the current state of our knowledge about the way in which the modern, complex, industrialized economy works.

But there would still be some pain. There would be some unemployment, but how much we cannot be sure. It would take a number of years for this policy to work itself out, years during which inflation, although falling, would still be running at an unpleasantly high level. It is certainly worth asking if there are not measures that might be taken to make this transition period as bearable as possible. A number of such measures are available and, as we shall now see, some are likely to be more effective than others.

Danger with unemployment benefits

It might seem reasonable for the government to do its utmost to ease the lot of those who find themselves unemployed during the transition to a lower inflation rate. If the authorities are deliberately going to undertake a policy that will generate some unemployment it seems only just to ensure that those who bear the brunt of this policy suffer as little as possible. There is certainly a strong case to be made along these lines, but there is a grave difficulty with it; the amount of unemployment in the economy is not independent of the level of support given to the unemployed. The frictional and structural unemployment we discussed above arises from workers taking time to acquire new skills and to find new jobs when they become unemployed. The higher is their living standard while not working, the more careful would one expect them to be about selecting a new job, and hence the longer they will take about it. This is not to say that the unemployed are shiftless, nor is it to argue for making unemployment as unpleasant a situation as possible. However, it is to say that the higher the level of unemployment benefits, the higher is likely to be the level of unemployment. This factor must be taken into account in deciding upon what level of support it would be appropriate to give to the unemployed as part of a general anti-inflation policy package.[9]

What about controls?

The discussion of the last few pages has laid heavy stress on the role of inflationary expectations in helping to generate unemployment during the transition to a lower inflation rate. We have already argued that if the government announces a credible anti-inflation policy, this in itself will contribute to a downward revision of expectations and to an easing of the unemployment problem during the transition. It is often argued that wage and price controls have just such an effect on expectations.[†] Controls certainly do not in, and of, themselves amount to an effective anti-inflation policy. It

---

[†]Editor's Note: On the effect of wage and price controls on expectations see Michael Parkin's essay in this volume.

does not follow from this, however, that they have no role to play as part of a broadly-based policy package that includes the all-important ingredient of monetary contraction. As with the question of increasing aid to the unemployed, so there is no definitive 'yes' or 'no' answer to be given to a proposal to use controls to influence inflationary expectations. If the public thinks such controls will contribute to slowing down inflation, then expectations will be favourably affected; if they don't then expectations will not be influenced.

There is some reason to believe that the introduction of controls had some transitory and minor effect on expectations in Britain in 1966 and in the U.S. in 1971; in Britain in 1972, however, their introduction seems to have had no discernible effect. Whether they will have any effect on expectations in Canada at the present time is anyone's guess. However, if the beneficial effect of controls is problematic, the harm that they might do is easier to discern. It has been seen in earlier chapters that controls can and do lead to all kinds of shortages and bottlenecks in the economy. Such effects as these lower the well-being of the community just as surely as do inflation and unemployment, and must be offset against any possible beneficial effects before an overall assessment of the likely contribution of wage and price controls to an anti-inflation package can be made. My own judgement is that controls would do more harm than good even if combined with a policy of monetary stringency.

Indexing

My assessment of policies that might directly contribute to the reduction of transitional unemployment, or make it more bearable for those who suffer it, is not then very encouraging. Things are a bit more hopeful when it comes to measures that might make inflation easier to live with while its rate is being slowly reduced. So called 'indexation' policies are often proposed to make life with inflation easier, policies that involve the automatic adjustment of the terms of contracts to compensate for changes in the cost of living.[10] There are three broad areas to which such measures could be applied — taxation and social security benefits, borrowing and lending, and wage agreements. The Canadian income tax already is indexed in a rough and ready way. Allowable deductions and the income bands to which particular tax rates are applied are adjusted year by year to take account of price level changes. Old age pensions and certain other social security benefits are also indexed. This policy surely makes an important contribution toward enabling Canadians to live with inflation more easily. At the moment, however, there is no indexation of capital gains taxation. If a man disposes of an asset whose market price has risen on a par with the cost of living, he has made no gain in real terms at all, but he is taxed as if he had. There is a strong case to be made, on grounds of fairness, for taxing capital gains only as they arise over and above changes in the general price level. A similar argument holds as far as the tax treatment of inventory appreciation of firms is concerned.[11]

Purchasing-power bonds

What about borrowing and lending? At present the rather high level of interest rates in the Canadian economy already reflect inflation to a good degree and compensate savers for its effects, but not completely. A small saver at a chartered bank or at a trust company is currently getting a return of seven to eight per cent. But with the inflation rate running at ten per cent he is actually paying two to three cents a year in real terms for every dollar of savings that he holds. If it is not intended to bring the inflation rate down quickly, there is a strong case to be made for the government making some kind of guaranteed purchasing power security available to small savers. Even a savings bond that promised to pay a rate of interest just equal to the inflation rate, and hence offered a zero real rate of return to its holders, would be better than any of the assets currently available to them. This is probably about as much as realistically could be accomplished along these lines. Government policy towards rates of return in the economy must be compatible with its policy towards the rate of monetary expansion. A gentle but sustained tightening up of money supply policy will produce some initial increase in interest rates followed by a downward trend in their levels as the inflation rate slows down. Given the background of such a monetary policy any attempt to introduce a widely available security which promised to pay a substantial rate of return as well as maintaining a guaranteed purchasing power would disrupt capital markets and bring with it the possibility of a much sharper contraction in real activity than the policies proposed in this chapter would engender. In short, not too much can be accomplished by introducing indexation into capital markets, but something could be done to protect small savers. Proposals to do something along these lines are well worth considering.

COLA clauses

Now let us turn to the final area to which indexation could be applied — to wage bargains. To the extent that inflationary expectations get built into wage contracts, the wage bargaining process already operates so as to provide members of the labour force with some protection against inflation. To propose to introduce cost of living, or COLA clauses as they are often called, into contracts is to suggest an alternative means of achieving the same end, and in one important respect this alternative means is also superior. Without escalator clauses, a proportion of negotiated wage increases are simply a compensation for expected increases in the price level. However, once negotiated, they must be paid, regardless of what actually happens to prices. This factor is, as we have already noted, an important contributor to the momentum that inflation generates, and hence a key element in the process whereby anti-inflation policy initially generates unemployment. The important point about escalator clauses is that they only lead to wage increases compensating for the cost of living *if* the cost of living actually does increase. The built-in momentum of inflation is reduced by their widespread use. A contractionary monetary policy that leads to a slowdown in the rate of price inflation will also immediately lead to a slowdown in wage inflation in the presence of escalator clauses. Hence it will generate less unemployment than it would were the time path of wage inflation already largely set by contracts negotiated before the policy was begun. Thus, the adoption of wage indexation would make it possible to reduce inflation at any given speed at a smaller cost in unemployment.

But what of the arguments that we sometimes hear that such indexation makes inflation worse by ensuring that price increases automatically become transformed into wage increases and thence to price increases again? Such arguments are valid against the background of an expansionary monetary policy. To adopt wage indexation and then to expand the rate of monetary expansion is to ensure as rapid as possible an acceleration in the inflation rate. Expectations of a relatively low inflation rate, built into long-term wage agreements, slow down the rate at which inflation can accelerate, just as expectations of high inflation slow down the rate at which it can be brought down. Wage indexation is a two-edged weapon. It can make sensible policies work more smoothly, but it can also do much to worsen the impact of inept policies. It is advocated here, therefore, not as a desirable policy in and of itself, but strictly as one component of an overall anti-inflation package.[12]

VII. SUMMARY

There is no easy and painless way of making the transition from double-digit inflation to price stability. The best that can be done is to proceed slowly, hence minimizing the unemployment that must inevitably accompany the transition. As to subsidiary measures that might smooth out the transition further, the most important is probably that the government clearly state its intentions in advance and then be seen to be following them through. This will have the effect of making the private sector's expectations about the future course of inflation compatible with government policy. Of subsidiary importance, but nevertheless worth implementing, would be an extension of already existing provisions to index taxation, the introduction of an indexed security tailored to the requirements of small savers, and the encouragement of the adoption of escalator clauses in wage contracts in the private sector. None of this would make the solution to the inflation problem painless but this is probably as good a programme as it is possible to devise in view of the current state of knowledge.

VIII. CONCLUSIONS

This chapter does not need a long concluding section. As stated at the outset, the proposals it outlines do not guarantee economic and social bliss, nor do they promise a rapid and painless cure for the Canadian economy's current problems. However, if they are implemented slowly, there is every reason to believe that they will produce a state of affairs much to be preferred to a continuation of the present situation. Though that present situation is serious, it is still relatively manageable compared to that ruling in other countries — Argentina and Britain for example. It is precisely because inflation is not yet doing any really lasting damage to the Canadian economy that the slow and relatively less painful cure for the disease proposed here is in fact such a practical proposition. The longer its implementation is delayed, the more deeply will inflation get built into the system, and the more difficult and painful will its cure become. Indeed, perhaps the greatest harm that controls will do to the Canadian economy lies in their distracting attention from, and delaying the implementation of, truly effective anti-inflation policies. By doing this they ensure that, when at last such policies are introduced, as introduced they eventually must be, their effects will be far more painful and disruptive than they would be were they to be set in motion now.

Notes

[1]The case for governing the behaviour of the money supply by a rule for its growth rate received its first comprehensive statement in Milton Friedman's, *Program for Monetary Stability*, New York, Fordham University Press, 1959. This chapter owes a considerable debt to that work.

[2]For a survey of the evidence on this matter the reader is referred to David Laidler, *The Demand for Money: Theories and Evidence*, Intext., Scranton, Pa., 1969, particularly Chapter 8. Studies of the Canadian economy that confirm the above conclusion include Carolyn Clark, "The Demand for Money and the Choice of a Permanent Income Estimate: Some Canadian Evidence 1926-65", *Journal of Money, Credit and Banking*, Aug. 1973, p. 733-93; T. Courchene and Alex K. Kelly, "Money Supply and Money Demand: An Econometric Analysis for Canada", *Journal of Money, Credit and Banking*, May 1971, p. 219-244.

[3]It is sometimes argued that the incentives which high interest rates give to people to economize on cash are sufficient to ensure that the tendency to built-in stability given by holding the rate of monetary expansion constant under discussion here is completely swamped. There is no evidence that this is the case. Cf. references given in footnote 2 above.

[4]Cf. p. 4-6 above.

[5]A further limit on the use of fiscal policy as a stabilization device would result from any inhibitions that the authorities might feel about encouraging capital inflows. Cf. p. 1-13 above.

[6]The level of unemployment which prevails when the economy is working at full capacity, but without there being any overall excess demand for labour, is often called the 'natural' unemployment rate. The phrase is Milton Friedman's. Cf. Milton Friedman, "The Role of Monetary Policy", *American Economic Review* 58, March 1968, p. 1-17.

[7]There is an extensive academic literature on the role of expectations in the inflationary process. For an up-to-date survey see David Laidler and Michael Parkin, "Inflation: A Survey", *Economic Journal*, December 1975, p. 1-69.

[8]For a study of the influence of unemployment and inflationary expectations on inflation in Canada see S. Kaliski, *The Trade-Off Between Inflation and Unemployment: Some Explorations of the Recent Evidence for Canada*, Ottawa, Economic Council of Canada Special Study No. 22, 1972.

[9]It has been estimated that the 1971 changes in unemployment benefits in Canada were responsible for .8 of a percentage point (or 14 per cent) of the unemployment rate in 1972. See H. Grubel, D. Maki and S. Sax, "Real and Insurance Induced Unemployment in Canada", *Canadian Journal of Economics*, May 1975, p. 174-191.

[10]A most readable discussion of the issues involved in indexation is to be found in H. Giersch et al., *Essays on Inflation and Indexation*, Washington, D.C. American Enterprise Institute for Public Policy Research, 1974.

[11]Not the least advantage of indexing taxation is that it forces the government to be honest. When it wishes to increase the real burden of taxation it has to take explicit action to do so. In the absence of indexation it simply allows inflation to push people into higher and higher tax brackets.

[12]One circumstance where indexation cannot and must not be applied is that involving a change in the world price of an important commodity such as oil or food. In such cases all consumers cannot be protected against the reduction in their living standard that must accompany a fundamental change in the price of one commodity relative to all others. If indexation is adopted, then an explicit adjustment would have to be made to account for such fundamental changes.

inflation dialogue

Inflation Dialogue

Some Questions And Answers About Inflation

MICHAEL WALKER

Chief Economist
The Fraser Institute

THE AUTHOR

Michael A. Walker, PhD., is Chief Economist of the Fraser Institute. Born in Newfoundland in 1945, he received his B.A. (Summa) at St. Francis Xavier University and his PhD. in Economics at the University of Western Ontario, 1969. From 1969 to 1973, he worked in various research capacities at the Bank of Canada, Ottawa and when he left in 1973, was Research Officer in charge of the Special Studies and Monetary Policy group in the Department of Banking. Immediately prior to joining the Fraser Institute, Dr. Walker was Econometric Model Consultant to the Federal Department of Finance, Ottawa.

Dr. Walker was Editor of, and a contributor to, the Fraser Institute's first publication "Rent Control - A Popular Paradox", published October, 1975.

Inflation Dialogue

Some Questions
And Answers
About Inflation

MICHAEL WALKER

Chief Economist
The Fraser Institute

I. INTRODUCTION

The purpose of this section is to summarize and extend the conclusions of this Fraser Institute book in the form of a dialogue. Readers undoubtedly will have had numerous questions occur to them as they read the book; probably there were places in the text where they parted company with the authors. There is a huge and subtle (and sometimes not so subtle) literature on the causes of inflation, the mechanisms of the inflationary process and the responses to inflation by governments, corporations, labour unions and the man in the street. And, in the final analysis, unless one leads a peculiarly cloistered existence, aren't we all persons in the street? For want of a better name, therefore, we have called the individual asking the questions (and sometimes answering them) Mr. Pits (Person-In-The-Street).† Mr. Pits assumes a number of identities which are more or less revealed by his stance on the issues discussed.

---

†Full credit must be given to the London Economist for originating the Pits family; as the family has not had its fortunes (and misfortunes) chronicled in the Economist for several years now, we would like the reader to assume that they emigrated.

In attempting to answer Mr. Pits' questions and to appreciate his reservations and pre-conceptions, we have drawn heavily from the conclusions of the various studies in this book as well as from other documented sources.

We warmly invite interested readers to continue the dialogue with us and we hope that some of this material will appear in future editions of the present work.

Let's invite Mr. Pits to put the first question.

II. ON THE CAUSE OF INFLATION

PITS: *So, summing it all up, what would you say is the real and fundamental cause of inflation?*

THE INSTITUTE: The direct cause of inflation is the creation of money by government at a faster rate than goods can be produced by the economy.

PITS: *I have heard that before; isn't that the old 'too many dollars chasing too few goods', argument? I thought that was discarded long ago as being an old wives tale?*

THE INSTITUTE: No, I don't think that it was ever discarded or discredited. The old saying was certainly very close to the truth, but it ignored the possibility that the increase in the number of dollars might, at least for a time, cause an increase in the number of goods. The government increases the number of dollars in circulation by increasing people's incomes. This increase may come either directly, in the form of transfer payments, or indirectly via government purchases of goods and services. To the people and the businesses who receive them the 'new' dollars are indistinguishable from 'old' dollars. The new dollars are accepted at the same value as 'old' dollars in spite of the fact that the new dollars may produce inflation and hence be worth less than 'old' dollars. Until the inflation process is well under way, people willingly sell their goods or services for the new dollars. Hence, in the beginning at least, the new dollars may cause real economic activity to increase.

The increase in total spending of dollars will call forth increased output of real goods and services if there is unused productive capacity. The businesses that first receive the dollars will increase their orders for goods since they will find their inventories running low and the firms that produce the goods will increase their output of goods to satisfy the increased demand. The problem that can arise is that dollars may be created by government faster than the capacity or ability of the economy as a whole to produce new goods. For example, if the output of goods from the firms affected by the initial increase in incomes is already at a very high level relative to capacity then the increase in demand for the goods will not produce, entirely, an increase in output but partially an increase in output and partially an increase in prices. The more readily the firm can sell its goods the less willing it is to give 'special deals' or 'volume discounts.' Beyond a certain point, increases in new dollar spending will encourage no more real output but only changes in the prices of goods. At this point, the old adage, 'too many dollars chasing too few goods', becomes a reasonably accurate description of the reality and of what is, at this point, the cause of inflation.

On the nature of Keynesian policies

PITS: *Ah, well it seems to me that what you are saying is: when the economy gets to 'full employment', increases in the money supply will cause a rise in prices. That is to say, once all of the resources of the economy are being fully-utilized and all of the people who want to work have jobs, then any further increase in money incomes beyond that point will have to be reflected solely in changes in price. But how can you say that is the current case when the unemployment rate is at its highest level since the 1930's?*

THE INSTITUTE: In order to give a satisfactory answer to that question, we have to trace our current policies back to their origins in the 1930's and in the theories of John Maynard Keynes. In 1934, when Keynes was writing his 'general theory', the world had just come through a period of financial collapse, falling prices and high and rising unemployment. The solution to the problem of unemployment then being suggested was a reduction in wages — i.e. deflation. Keynes correctly saw that in the then existing circumstances wage cuts would not produce the desired result because of the effect that the lower level of incomes would have on spending and on confidence. Keynes accordingly proposed an inflationary policy designed to boost employment (via public works) and money incomes directly, in the hope that thereby investor confidence and private sector employment would be given a boost. The solution that Keynes proposed to the problem of the 1930's embodied in it the view that inflation did not matter:

> "the important thing to say was that deflation would not help. It was right, then; but it was not the whole story. To have made it into a general principle, working both ways, was surely (we must now say) very unfortunate."†

In other words, the Keynesian cure was designed to overcome a specific set of problems — it is not a generally applicable solution.

In order to illustrate the nature of the Keynesian solution consider the position of an old-fashioned hamburger stand next door to one of the new mass-production hamburger stands. The old-fashioned hamburger stand can't sell hamburgers at as low a price as the modern one simply because its costs per hamburger are higher. The old stand will find, ultimately, that its business will disappear because its prices are higher than those at the new stand.

However, on Saturdays the number of people who want hamburgers is so high that queues begin to form at the new hamburger stand. Since this means that people must wait longer for their hamburgers, and their time is worth something, they are effectively paying a higher price. The old stand with its higher prices and no waiting now seems attractive to people again.

The point is that during the week when demand is low the old stand can't compete and this would cause the stand to go out of business and the proprietor to find a new job. This would not happen if 'everyday were a Saturday' when hamburger demand is at a peak. If the demand for hamburgers was kept at the Saturday level every day in the week then the old stand could remain in business — even though its costs were not competitive with the modern stand.

Of course, after a while either the modern stand would expand or another modern stand would open. In the final analysis, even 'Saturday every day' won't help the old-style hamburger stand.

---

†John Hicks, *The Crisis in Keynesian Economics*, Basil Blackwell, Oxford, 1974, page 62.

The lesson is that even if an operation is inherently uneconomic, growth in demand can, in the short-run, disguise its inefficiency. Thereby, the growth in demand may sustain a firm and the jobs it provides in an industry long after it has outlived its efficient life. The firm and the employment provided are thus dependent on the continual expansion of demand.

The Keynesian solution to the problem of unemployment is very similar to the 'Saturday every day' solution to the hamburger stand's problem. It should be clear that the underlying problem is not being solved although the immediate problem is being overcome. In the final analysis the problem will not be solved until the old stand has been shut down or more investment in it has been made to change the relative structure of cost and operating revenues.

For an economy as a whole, the more relative imbalances of this sort that exist the higher must the rate of growth of money spending be to overcome them. It is also unfortunately the case that different sectors of the economy reach full capacity at different levels of output. Therefore, it is quite possible to have effectively reached the capacity output of the economy before sufficient demand pressure has been produced to overcome the imbalances in a particular sector. In terms of the one resource that you focussed on, i.e. the labour force, it is quite conceivable that the economy as a whole will be starting to inflate before full employment of the labour force has been achieved.

The rate of unemployment at which the general inflation begins has been called the natural rate of unemployment to indicate that it is the highest rate of employment — the lowest rate of unemployment — that can be achieved simply by increasing demand pressure. Increases in the pressure of demand beyond the natural rate of unemployment will not produce further decreases in the rate of unemployment, but will only produce inflation. Keynes could (consciously) ignore this aspect of his 'solution' because, for a variety of reasons, the rate of unemployment in the 1930's was far above the 'natural' rate.

On the natural rate of unemployment

PITS: *Well, although you argue convincingly, you certainly have got a lot of nerve to talk about 8 per cent unemployment as being the natural rate of unemployment. It seems to me that there is nothing very natural about it — particularly for those who are unemployed.*

THE INSTITUTE: I accept your point; I should perhaps use the term 'natural' advisedly. What I mean is that given all the structural characteristics of the economy, for example, the extent of union power, the extent of government expenditure as a proportion of total spending, the level of unemployment insurance benefits and so on, there is a rate of unemployment that in the long-run it would not be possible to go below using demand pressure as the policy instrument to achieve a lower level.

Sometimes economists distinguish between what can be accomplished in the short-term and what can be accomplished in the long-term. In terms of the natural rate of unemployment a growing number of economists are coming to believe that it is only possible to achieve a level of unemployment below the natural rate in the short-run. This can be achieved only because the increases in money demand by government *appear* to be increases in real demand. However, after people have learned that they are not real increases in spending, the level of employment will fall back down to the natural rate. In terms of a familiar concept of a few years ago, economists say that there is a trade-off in the short-run but no trade-off in the long-run between unemployment and inflation. In the long-term, inflation does not reduce unemployment.

PITS: *How does all of this fit in with what I see going on around me every day? The unbelievable wages that people are demanding — and getting — for what would only a few years ago have been regarded as unskilled labour. There doesn't seem to be any 'rhyme or reason' to the relative rates of pay any more. Is that all part of the 'natural' unemployment concept?*

THE INSTITUTE: The reason people can demand and receive what seem to be very high wages is to be found in the general inflation itself. The employer, for his part, is willing to pay higher wages because he expects to be able to 'pass on' his costs in higher prices. In an environment where the government is artificially boosting spending by increasing the money supply, employers will be able to pass on their costs because initially consumers don't cut their expenditures when the prices start to rise.

The employee, on the other hand, is led to believe, by his successful demands, that his services are becoming more and more valuable. And, as long as the government keeps increasing the level of dollar spending, the employee will continue to find employment at the very high wages to which by now he has grown accustomed.

In all of this, the question of how much the services of a postal worker, a manual labourer or an engineer are 'really' worth becomes lost. The possibility of making accurate calculations of relative worth or value is lost in the haze created by the increasing money price of everything. Everybody expects both prices and wages to rise, so workers demand higher wages and employers are willing to pay them.

At the base of the whole process is the artificial maintenance of total spending by government. Wages are ultimately paid by the consumer who spends to buy the product or service. If total spending is artificially maintained then prices and wages can rise at an artificially high rate.

On inflation and union power

PITS: *Well, you have argued your case very strongly; however, I still find it very difficult to accept. For example, I find it very difficult to believe that unions are not at the base of this whole problem and that if we broke the power of the unions then we would stop inflation.*

THE INSTITUTE: I can sympathize with your uneasiness about my explanation, at least to the extent that it is very easy to understand how people or why people think unions produce inflation. From the point of view of the Canadian businessman, wages, on average, form his biggest single cost and accordingly, wages have a very significant effect on his cost structure. Since he then reflects these higher costs in higher prices, it is easy to see why he might feel that unions cause inflation. However, what power does the businessman have to ensure that he can charge the higher price that higher costs imply? Can he 'extort' the higher price from the market in the same way that higher wages were 'extorted' from his firm? Of course, he cannot.

Some firms may be able to raise their prices without effect because the demand for their products is relatively insensitive to changes in price. However, most firms will find that an increase in the price of their product leads to a reduction in the amount of the product that they can sell — relative to the amount that they could have sold at a lower price. (For example, products that are sold on a world market become relatively more expensive and hence cannot be sold.) The inability to sell as much implies an inability to produce as much and correspondingly means less employment for the workers whose wages have just been increased.

In other words, although a successful, high wage demand may produce a higher price for a particular product, it does so by causing less output of that product and less employment than would otherwise have occurred.

Since there is less employment and less output, there will be less of a demand on the total productive capacity of the country. Ultimately, this excess capacity will have an effect on the prices of other products. The net effect of the increase in wages is likely to be no change in the average rate of price increase (some prices will rise less rapidly than they would have while others rise more).

PITS: *Well, I don't like to be impolite, but I think that that is the biggest bunch of nonsense that I have ever heard. When the firm gives the workers a raise the workers all have more money. When they spend the money they push up the demand for all products. That is why the firms can keep raising their prices and why the whole spiral keeps going and going and going.*

THE INSTITUTE: It is easy to become tangled in one's own snare in all of this. First of all, I suppose that you would admit that a wage gain higher than that warranted by productivity will, soon or late, cause a loss of jobs. Given that that is the case, it is not at all clear that total spending will grow to keep up with the price increases that wage gains cause. In fact, if there is no external economic pressure applied to the circumstances that we are talking about, it is unlikely that total spending would rise. It is more likely that total spending would stay about the same with fewer workers spending a higher wage. Of course, this assumes that no outside economic pressure is applied.

In point of fact, outside economic pressure is applied in

the form of increases in government spending financed by increases in the money supply. Increases in money spending that can only cause further inflation in the long-term prevents the rise in wages from having its natural consequence in the short-term. Total spending rises as a result of increased monetary growth — government validates and makes possible an inflationary spiral that would not be possible in the absence of government action to increase the money supply.

A more direct linkage between wage demands and the inflation process can be found in civil service unions. The ultimate check on the ability of unions to extract uneconomic wages is the necessity that the firm cover its costs. In the case of government — as is by now common knowledge — no such constraint exists. Governments can simply run a deficit and finance it by borrowing or creating more money. Since civil service wage claims are not subjected to the 'market test' they can form the core of a particularly insidious 'spiral'.

If wage claims by the civil service result in higher wages, this will produce, via inter-union equity claims, a demand for higher wages in the private sector. The subsequent threat of unemployment may cause the government to further increase its spending and the money supply. This, in turn, permits the higher level of prices implied by the higher wage demands.

PITS: *Ah, so you admit that unions can cause inflation, if only indirectly. If that is the case then you must agree that wage and price controls are a good policy to deal with that problem.*

THE INSTITUTE: No, I would not agree that I have admitted to the inflationary consequences of unionism. I have said that is conceivable that high unemployment may cause government to produce money at a faster rate than it otherwise would have. I have also agreed that unions can produce unemployment. I have not agreed that the inflationary period in which we currently live has been produced by unions. In that regard, if we examine the period of the last fifteen years, it is not at all clear that the rate of increase in wages achieved by unions has led the increase in the money supply and led the increase in prices. In fact, the historical record for Canada is more consistent with the view that the

Table 1

Unions, Money Supply and Inflation
Canada 1960-1975

Year	Percentage Increase in Labour Income per Unit of Output*	Average for the Period	Percentage Increase in the Consumer Price Index	Average for the Period	Percentage Change in the Extent of Unionization of the Labour Force	Average for the Period	Percentage Increase in the Money Supply	Average for the Period
1960	2.3		1.3		-2.1		4.6	
1961	1.3		.2		-3.8		8.6	
1962	.1	1.5	1.6	1.4	-1.8	-1.6	3.8	6.2
1963	1.4		1.8		-0.5		6.4	
1964	2.2		1.9		0.0		7.4	
1965	4.2		2.9		4.0		12.0	
1966	5.7		3.6		5.6		6.5	
1967	7.2	5.3	4.1	4.7	6.5	3.4	15.9	11.9
1968	2.9		4.1		1.9		13.3	
1969	6.3		4.6		-1.1		3.9	
1970	5.8	5.8	1.5	1.5	3.4	3.4	10.8	3.9
1971	4.0		5.0		-1.5		14.9	
1972	5.2	5.1	5.1	6.4	3.0	2.7	15.9	15.0
1973	6.1		9.1		6.5		18.3	
1974	13.8	13.4	12.4	11.4	0.0	0.5	16.8	17.0
1975	13.1		10.4		1.0		17.1	

Sources: *Labour Organizations in Canada*, Labour-Canada, 1974-1975, Table 1. Bank of *Canada Review*, January 1976, Tables 51, 52.

*Note: Labour income per unit of output is the national accounts measure of total labour income divided by total output as measured by GNP in constant dollars.

rate of increase in the money supply, due to a high rate of growth of government expenditure, produced inflation which led to very high rates of wage demands by unions.

In any event, if it were true that unions were the cause of inflation via the unemployment that union power creates, the appropriate way to deal with that is through changes in the legislation which affect unions, i.e. directly and not indirectly via a disruptive set of controls such as those which have been adopted by the Canadian government. Thus, even if I did agree with your conclusion about unions and the money supply, I would not agree that it follows that wage and price controls are the appropriate policy to deal with the problem.

I have assembled a table of data (Table 1) on the question of labour cost, unionism and inflation and the story it tells is very interesting. For example, it indicates that during the period immediately prior to the current inflationary explosion (1971-1973) 'union power' on average, and labour costs per unit of output grew less rapidly than they had during the preceeding six years. It was not until the inflation explosion had begun that unit labour costs began to grow more rapidly. 'Union power', on the other hand, seems to have steadily weakened from its peak growth period in the late sixties.

During the period 1960-1965, which was a period of monetary stability, prices and labour cost per unit of output both grew at modest rates and the extent of 'union power' actually declined. The inflation that was produced by the money supply growth during the 1965-1969 period was reflected both in higher labour costs and in an increase in the growth of 'union power'.

If 'union power' did directly produce inflation one would expect a surge in union power to precede a surge in the inflation rate. Or if the chain of causality from union power to unemployment to political fear to money printing is supposed to be operational then, one would expect to find surges in 'union power' to precede increases in the money supply and this to be followed by a surge in the inflation rate. An inspection of the data in Table 1 does not support either of these statements regarding the effects of union power.

Of course, this treatment of the union power question may be regarded as highly unsatisfactory since over the period examined there have been changes in the legislation concerning unions' ability to engage in restrictive practices. Accordingly, the fact, for example, that the proportion of the labour force unionized actually fell in 1971 may not be a good indicator of the change in the extent of union power. However, to the extent that the omission of legislative changes from the data detracts from the current analysis, it adds to the case for dealing with union power by direct legislative action rather than with the clumsy device of wage and price controls.

PITS: *From a purely academic point of view it is true that the way to deal with union power is via changes in the law. But such changes are unlikely in the near future, and wage controls imposed by government do a good job of forcing unions to accept reasonable settlements.*

THE INSTITUTE: From your attitude I'd say that you are a businessman who faces a large, powerful union. You probably have negotiations coming up this year and are worried that the union is going to extract a large settlement.

PITS: *Yes, that's right.*

THE INSTITUTE: I understand the position you find yourself in and I know that collective bargaining can be a very trying process. However, I think that you are too quick to embrace controls as the solution to your problem. Controls can have a consequence for your bargaining position that I am sure you would not find attractive.

For example, suppose that the union with which you have to negotiate decides not to accept the ruling of the anti-inflation board. Suppose they decide to confront the government by refusing to work at wages that are within the guidelines? In that event, the union will be negotiating with the government and you, as an employer, will have no control over the resolution of the matter.

It may be that this possibility doesn't worry you right now, but if the union that you are worried about really has got a lot of power, you should worry. If the union is powerful it may decide that it can confront the government and you could find yourself in bankruptcy while the government digs in its toes. Unless you are prepared to be involved in a 'test case' where the government is determined to 'show good example' you had better reconsider your position.

The cases of Chrysler and the coal industry in the U.K. are good examples of what can happen to firms that get caught in the union-government nut-cracker that is produced by controls. The evidence from the U.K. suggests that, far from solving the problem of union power, controls make its effects more difficult to deal with.

On government spending and inflation

PITS: *I know that your solution to the problem is to reduce the growth in the money supply and I have some questions about that later. For now, I want to ask you about government expenditures. Next to union power, I think that the biggest cause of inflation is government spending. Governments are spending more and more money every year and absorbing a larger and larger share of the total output of the economy. Surely this must produce inflation even if the government borrows or taxes to get the money to increase its expenditures.*

THE INSTITUTE: It doesn't look as though we are going to be able to totally agree about anything in this conversation. I am afraid that I can only partly agree with your opinions about government expenditure and inflation. In order to demonstrate the nature of my disagreement, I want to consider a particular circumstance.

Suppose that the whole economy consisted of one small town and that the government was proposing to build a retraining centre for defunct economists. In order to get the money to build the centre the government decided to raise the property tax rate. During the time that the centre was being built, if we were monitoring the situation with a system of national accounts, we would observe that government expenditure had increased by an amount equal to the expenditures being made on the centre and all the other expenditures in the town would have gone down by about the same amount. The reason is that if people's incomes had not changed, the increase in the tax rate would mean that people had less income after tax to spend and hence would do less spending in total. Unless the total income and spending in the community changed, the increase in government expenditure has to be financed by getting money from the citizens.

It follows that if the citizens give up some of their money either via increased taxes or by lending to the government then they have less money to spend themselves.

PITS: *Ah, I agree in the short-run that is probably what does happen, and that there isn't any inflationary impact of government in the short-run. However, to the extent that government borrows or taxes to provide the community with creature comforts (retraining centre) the community does not have the capital to invest in productive capacity. Therefore, the productive capacity of the community as a whole falls and in the long-term this will lead to inflation because the productivity of the community will be less than it would have been.*

THE INSTITUTE: Yes, I agree that in the long-term the allocation of expenditures by government does reduce the productive capacity of the economy and ultimately this can produce inflation. However, it will only do so to the extent that government continuously replaces productive investments with 'non-productive' ones and does so at an increasing rate.

The effect of building a retraining centre instead of making a productive investment will wear off in time in the same way that the productive investment would have worn out. A 'one-shot' replacement of productive capital cannot be claimed to have a permanent effect on productivity and hence prices. If the government proceeded indefinitely to build retraining centres for other defunct scientists then it would have a sustained negative effect on productivity and hence a sustained effect on prices. Prices would be higher than they would have been.

If the government engaged in such a sweeping program of taxation and expenditure that the total amount of productive capacity being replaced in each year was growing, then the government would be producing inflation. That is, the negative effect of government on productivity and hence the positive effect on prices would be growing year by year.

Since the latter situation describes the Canadian government's behaviour in recent times, I would have to agree with your conclusion about the effect of governments on productivity. To the extent that governments replace and suppress productive investments, they reduce the ability of the economy to respond to the demands that government encourages the population to make of it. It is this backdrop of increasing demand that causes the capital suppressing activity of the government to produce inflation.

On the price of oil and inflation

PITS: *Well, there's one thing for sure that I know and that is that at least partly the current inflation that we have is due to the Arabs restricting the supply of oil and pushing its price up astronomically.*

THE INSTITUTE: Well, in believing that you are at least in good company since it appears that a very great number of people think that the OPEC increase in the price of oil caused at least some of our current inflationary problems. On the surface it is very easy to understand why many people think that increasing oil costs imply increasing inflation. In the first place, oil is a so-called basic commodity and hence has an impact on a very great number of the things that we use in our everyday lives. It makes sense that an increase in the price of such a basic commodity would, therefore, produce an increase in the price of the commodities that depend upon it.

In order to get at the kernel of truth in the foregoing remark it is necessary to strip away the 'veil' of money that surrounds the transaction. Essentially, when Canada imports oil from the Middle East or from elsewhere, it is offering goods in exchange for oil. When the Arabs colluded to restrict the supply of oil they essentially said to Canadians and to other countries, "we want more goods in exchange for our oil — thirty fridges for one thousand barrels of oil instead of ten fridges." From the rest of the world's point of view, this essentially meant that in order to maintain the consumption of oil at its previous level the rest of the world had to give up more goods in exchange. Overnight the standard of living of the rest of the world was reduced at the expense of an increase in the standard of living of the Arabs.

It is very clear, however, that this was a once and for all change in the relative standard of living of the oil producing and non-oil producing sectors of the world. Accordingly, the increase in the price of oil and in the price of oil-dependent commodities was a once and for all price increase. It is clear that there is no continuing rise in the price of oil and other commodities implied by the OPEC cartel's increase in the price of oil. This fact notwithstanding, it is possible that the multi-stage world-wide adjustment to the changed price of oil could appear like a general inflation. However, in the absence of a change in other factors, the increase in the price of oil must imply smaller expenditures on and hence smaller increases in the prices of other commodities. The process of adjustment to a higher price for oil will obviously involve some reduction in the consumption of oil and some reduction in the consumption of other commodities. (The movement to smaller cars is a reflection of this process — less money spent on cars and greater gas mileage, hence less money spent on gas.)

There is, however, a set of policy responses to this oil price adjustment procedure that could produce a generalized inflation. Namely, an attempt by government to cover up the reduction in real incomes implied by the change in the price of oil. In order to illustrate what I mean I will use as an example a state of affairs similar to the current one and in which, with the benefit of hindsight, we are able to analyze cause and effect. The circumstance I have in mind is that of the reparation payments following the First World War which are very similar to the current transfer of wealth from the non-oil producing countries to the oil producing countries in OPEC.

Essentially the reparation payments following the First World War were an attempt by Lloyd George and his colleagues at Versailles to extract from Germany the full cost of the First World War. Germany was to pay this cost by transferring resources to the victors. The payment was to be in the form of currency and commodities and a schedule of payment was laid down in very precise terms.

The terms of that reparation agreement were so severe that, in effect, it was not politically possible for the German government to withstand their impact. In order to put the recent Arab oil payments in perspective, it should be noted that the reparation payments that Germany was to pay in the first year amounted to five billion dollars — an amount equal to, at that time, about one quarter of the total investment that Britain had abroad. About a year later a further reparation indemnity of 32 billion dollars was assessed. Relatively speaking, the oil payments to the Arabs from any one country are modest compared to the kind of figures we are now talking about. However, the response by the government of Germany in the 1920's was very similar to the response in the 1970's by most of the countries who import oil from the OPEC countries.

Basically, the reaction of the oil importing countries has been not to permit the reduction in real incomes caused by the increase in the real price of oil. In the case of Canada, this has involved an attempt to maintain a two price system for oil — exporting and importing at one price and consuming at another lower price. The two price system has been maintained by the government via subsidies on the price of imported oil to bring it down to the cost of domestic oil.

In the case of the German reparation payments the German government attempted to pay the reparation payments, not by taxing or by reducing the real standard of living of the German citizenry, but by simply increasing the rate at which it printed money. Effectively, the government ran a continuous deficit equal to the amount of the reparation payments due.

Needless to say, this led to a very dramatic decline in the value of the German currency and to the hyper-inflation of which we have all heard. The German mark, which had a par value of 23.8 cents American, was worth only .3 cents in November 1921. By November 1923, the value of the mark had fallen to the meaningless level of .0000000002 cents.

One economic historian has summarized the case as follows:

> "This financial collapse was due primarily to the continual refusal of the German government to make any approach towards a balanced budget and not to the demand for reparation payments, though this, of course, affected what was politically possible . . ."†

The Canadian situation is similar in the sense that the government is using tax revenues to subsidize oil use and suppressing rises in the price of crude oil in order to temporarily prevent the market price of oil from rising. (An insane aspect of the situation is that the government is also spending money to convince people to economize on oil. In other words, the government is making oil less expensive so

---

†William Ashworth, *The International Economy Since 1850*, Longmans, Second Edition, 1962, p. 244.

that people can afford to buy more and at the same time is trying to discourage people from using oil.) The government is subsidizing oil for political reasons in an attempt to isolate the Canadian people from the reality that they must soon face. The cash that is used to subsidize oil gives rise to a larger cash requirement and hence, more money creation by government.

Thus, on a smaller scale, the government is using the age-old 'trick' of money creation to attempt to cover up what is a basic change in circumstances for Canadians. It was precisely this illusion, carried to extremes, that produced the German hyper-inflation.

III. ON WAGE AND PRICE CONTROLS

PITS: *Well, you say that you wouldn't adopt a system of wage and price controls, but isn't it true that wage and price controls have worked in the United States and the United Kingdom?*

THE INSTITUTE: The quick answer to your question is no, wage and price controls have not worked by and large. It is true that during one peace - time application of controls in the United Kingdom they did appear to have some shock effect on the rate of inflation. They also appear to have had a modest effect during the Phase I of President Nixon's Economic Stabilization Program. However, the overall evidence from the United Kingdom indicates that wage and price controls have had no effect on the overall long term rate of inflation and have served only to distract public and government attention away from the true cause of the inflation, which has been the rapid rate of money supply creation. In the U.S., as Michael Darby points out in his study in this volume, the principal effect of the controls seems to have been a reduction in the quality of goods and no real reduction in the rate at which true prices were rising.

Wage and price controls can fool people into thinking that neither wages nor prices are rising. For example, it may be that during a particular control period the wages of a Class I carpenter have not changed or have risen only at the specified control rate. However, if during that period there was a 20 per cent increase in the number of Class II carpenters who are paid a higher wage, then effectively the overall wage for carpenters has risen. On the price side, if the quality of the products has been reduced or if products are sold in a different form than they were before controls were imposed, then a true increase in price may be hidden. For example, the price of gasoline may not change at all during a particular period, but owing to shortages the average waiting time in line to fill up with gas may have increased from several minutes to an hour or more. Effectively, this means that the price of gasoline has risen to the consumer, but this price increase will never be reflected in the official numbers.

Because of these and other such effects Professor Darby and others have concluded that wage and price controls do not reduce inflation, but may create an illusion of a reduction in the rate of inflation because price and wage increases are hidden. Because of effects similar to these it is also to be doubted whether wage and price controls even worked during a period of high patriotic commitment to national goals such as the Second World War. Certainly the analysis contained in this volume about the Canadian experience during the war would indicate that wage and price controls had very little effect on the true rate of inflation.

IV. ON THE SOLUTION

PITS: *Well, then what is your solution to the problem ? From what you said I take it you would simply reduce the rate of growth of money supply. Is that right?*

THE INSTITUTE: Yes, our solution to the problem is that the Department of Finance not permit the total money supply to grow at a rate faster than the rate at which the Canadian economy can produce new output of goods.

PITS: *Well, if I read the situation properly it seems to me that what you are calling for is a 50 per cent or more reduction in the rate at which the money supply is growing?*

THE INSTITUTE: Yes, that is right.

On the costs of the cure

PITS: *Well, that seems to me to be absurd. Wouldn't that produce the most horrendous consequences in terms of the unemployment rate and in terms of bankruptcies and all sorts of financial calamities?*

THE INSTITUTE: Certainly that is what many people would like you to believe. Prime Minister Trudeau wanted to

233

convey that impression to people in his, by now famous, control speech. Similarly, one can find rumours of that sort of position in the remarks of the Governor of the Bank of Canada. However, the fact is that during 1960 to 1964 the money supply in Canada grew at about the rate I am suggesting.

It is no more unrealistic to suggest that the money supply ought to grow at the same rate it grew then than it is to suggest that the money supply be allowed to continue to grow and to continue to produce the double-digit inflation that we have today. Besides, it is easy to exaggerate the effect that a reduction in the rate of growth of money supply would have on the rate of unemployment. For example, during the famous hyperinflation of 1923-1924 in Germany, there was a drastic reduction in the rate of money supply production. In the beginning of January, 1924, government departments at all levels were told that they could have no more money to compensate for inflationary cost rises. This produced a very large increase in unemployment. From October 1923 to January 1924 the number of unemployed rose from 1.2 million to 2 million. The spectacular thing about it is that by the following June, that is June 1924, the number of people unemployed had fallen to 600,000.†

PITS: *In other words, what you are saying is that although the reduction in the rate of inflation implies an increase in unemployment, you are willing to accept the increase in unemployment that will occur. Isn't that a rather harsh and unrealistic attitude to take? Wouldn't it be better to continue to expand the money supply, hence produce some inflation, but use wage and price controls to keep inflation 'under control' and keep the rate of unemployment low?*

THE INSTITUTE: Ah yes, I think I can see what you mean. You mean let us try and live with inflation. Try, in effect, to use wage and price controls to capture the benefits of inflation without its costs. Then as firm after firm and industry after industry becomes non-competitive and unable to operate at a profit the government could simply nationalize them. And of course, government could always create new industry for example, heavy water plants, pulp and paper mills, electronics industries, airplane manufacturing plants.

---

†We are indebted to A.A. Walters for drawing this point to our attention.

I am afraid that what you are proposing is exactly the problem that we have. There can be no doubt that our current problems are related to the attempt over the past 20 years by government in Canada to create artificial pockets of employment where no natural tendency in that direction existed. There can be no doubt that the co-existence in the Atlantic provinces of a very high rate of unemployment and a very high rate of government pump priming over a very long period of time reflect on the inability of government to produce a permanent change in the employment structure. Inflationary government expenditure cannot solve an employment problem. It can only, by pressure, overcome it in the short-term. Unfortunately, in the process of overcoming an existing employment problem, the pressure of demand creates a whole array of artificial jobs as well. Also, to the extent that people are fooled by the inflationary bulge in demand, the demand pressure creates false expectations. For example, in a depressed area bolstered by a government contract or bolstered by an undue level of artificial government demand for a product, support industries grow up and secondary levels of employment become dependent on the inflationary level of expenditures. To the extent that government expenditures generate this sort of investment and employment, it produces the possibility that when the final correction has to be made the resulting level of unemployment will be much higher than it would normally have been.

We cannot pretend that it will be possible forever to maintain an employment situation out of keeping with the economic realities. The choice is not that between inflation now and unemployment now, but between unemployment now and unemployment later. Since pursuing our current course is likely to produce a much higher unemployment rate later, when the final correction is made, the Fraser Institute is in favour of a policy that would see the rate of growth of the money supply return to the level at which it was during the early 1960's.

It is worth noting, incidentally, that during the period 1961-1965 the rate of unemployment was at a low average level relative to our recent experience. Canada did not benefit much, unemployment-wise, from the rapid expansion of the money supply from 1965 onwards. The unemployment rate did dip down to historically low figures in 1966 and 1967 but from 1968 onwards it was higher than it had been, on average, over the 1961-1965 period. Currently the unemployment rate is higher than it has been since the depression — a legacy of the monetary and fiscal policies that have been adopted for the last ten years in Canada.

PITS: *I must say that your logic is convincing but my feelings are very much against your conclusions. Isn't your preoccupation with inflation a purely upper middle class concern? The people that are unemployed — mostly lower middle class and minority groups — would be prepared to live with a lot more inflation than we currently have if only they could get a job. Shouldn't the objective be full employment at any price?*

THE INSTITUTE: Your last statement summarizes the guiding principle of economic policy in Britain, and to a lesser extent, the U.S. and Canada during the past thirty years. Perhaps we can best answer your question by quoting to you something that appeared in the London (England) Daily Telegraph the other day (January 24, 1976):

> "Unemployment follows inevitably from inflation at anything like the rate we have experienced in 1975. Inflation is the cause and unemployment is the result . . . if you say you do not care about inflation and only about unemployment you will end up with both uncontrollable inflation and still worse unemployment."

That was a statement of Mr. Roy Jenkins, Secretary of State for the Home Department — a Minister in a British Labour government and, until recently, a man commited to the notion that full employment must be pursued at all cost. One could scarcely hope to find more damning evidence against the policies that you recommend than to find that where (Britain) they have been most vigorously pursued they have produced disaster.